I0137506

THE WORLD OF TOMORROW

THE TEACHERS OF THE HIGHER PLANES
Fifth Book of Wisdom

Ruth Lee, *Scribe*

LeeWay
PUBLISHING

Copyright © 2016 by Ruth Lee. All rights reserved. No portion of this book may be reproduced mechanically, electronically, or by any other means, including photocopying, without written permission of the publisher. It is illegal to copy this book, post it to a website, or distribute it by any other means without permission from the author.

This book is an updated and revised version of the 2006 edition originally published by AuthorHouse

LeeWay Publishing
Naples, FL www.LeeWayPublishing.com

ISBN: 978-0-9970529-4-7
Library of Congress Control Number: 2016959076
Printed in the United States of America First Printing 2016

Cover design by Sarah Barrie of Cyanotype.ca
Internal design by Alfredo Sarraga Jr.

More Books by **Ruth Lee**

Dedicated to seekers of wisdom and those delving
into the mysteries of spirituality for the first time

Introduction

LeeWay Publishing was created to reproduce works channeled by the extraordinary spiritual scribe, Ruth Lee, otherwise known as *The Scribe*. She alone supervised the republication of **The World of Tomorrow,** the fifth volume in *The Books of Wisdom* series, in a new format and style—without making significant changes to the original channeled manuscript.

Why was Ruth Lee chosen to 'scribe' The Books of Wisdom?

In 1993, a group of teachers from another space and time identified themselves simply as *The Teachers of The Higher Planes* and selected Ruth Lee to trance-scribe *The Books of Wisdom*, including **The World of Tomorrow.** She agreed to diligently reproduce their dictation, as a good scribe does, but refused to be held responsible for interpreting their work later. Once Ruth Lee accepted this assignment, she never questioned *The Teachers* or asked about their mission. That is why she is their scribe and others are not!

The Teachers have this to say about their first work on Earth: "You can read these books in any sequence and still not achieve wisdom, yet we call these efforts *The Books of Wisdom*. If you read each book, will you achieve immortality? Actually, you are already immortal. However, some might stay in the world so long they become immoral, thus unable to achieve a life beyond the one lived now. We would not want that to happen, but you are allowed to fail at life. You have free will to do anything you like this life. However, life is a lot better on the higher planes. Believe us--and pass the tests as presented."

It is the hope of *The Teachers of the Higher Planes* and Ruth Lee working as their scribe that each reader finds clues, if not answers, to many of this life's mysteries. **The World of Tomorrow** provides many answers, but as always, it is up to the reader to determine whether or not to heed *The Teachers'* instructions and advice.

THE WORLD OF TOMORROW

THE TEACHERS OF THE HIGHER PLANES
Fifth Book of Wisdom

Ruth Lee, *Scribe*

LeeWay
PUBLISHING

THE WORLD OF TOMORROW

Chapter One

When you look at the stars you can see you are not alone in the universe, but where are you? Where do you belong in the entire scheme of things? What is your place and where are you going now? These questions continue to plague or intrigue wise men and women, but seldom thought through once a person becomes established in the world. Why is that?

The only person who questions you is You, your Higher Self. All others are disinterested in the final outcome of your life here. They have their lives to concentrate on and are held accountable for them when the end of all these Earthly concerns arrives—be sure you, too, know the answers to the important questions of your life.

If you are the only one in your family, you have no family—only ancestry. To have no family implies you have no roots, but you do. You are the end-product of one entire outgrowth of a much larger entity of the universe, known here simply as YOU. You are not the entire universe, but you have it within YOU.

When you decided to appear on Earth in human form, you also decided to bring along with you Spiritual Guides from other aspects of your entire personality or entity to help you while here. Those beings are of You (your Higher Self) and exist within *you*, but you are not the only one here. Your Guides also have *'personalities'* of their own which are led through difficult passages by other, higher Spiritual Guides in order to accelerate their learning and advancement, too.

What if you are here alone?

What if God had forsaken you at the time you were born into human form? What do you think would have happened? You never contemplate such questions, because you know within *you* that you are not alone and that God will never forsake you—so act like it!

Now that your life on Earth is maturing—possibly ending, you need to think of where you will go next. You need several things to prepare for the transition before you can move forward. What will you need for this transition, and how best can you hasten it? You need a clear conscience and a pure heart, but what else? Several other attributes are also required. What are they?

- A long life of service to others.
- A list of what you can do.
- A series of experiences that predict your ability to transfer attributes from one life to another or one existence to another;
- You need to totally understand the process of living this life, in order to process information as rapidly as possible.

All of these attributes are not of You, but within the human being *you* are now.

You need never fear another human being, but you will. You will fear others as long as you live on Earth—only to discover later that they feared you! Why all this confusion and fear? It goes with the territory. You came here to identify and learn to cope with such emotions and conditions, but have no need to be overwhelmed or absorbed by them. You choose to do that to yourself!

In the course of preparing this material for your study, we looked at all there is to know while you are on Earth and found significant areas of misunderstanding. Most surround what you need to know to progress to the next plane once this life is over, as well as where you will then go within your eternal being.

You should know by this time that we do not vindicate nor condone earthly practices that enslave or hinder you from developing as far as you can go while on Earth. It is you who choose to do so. Why? You love being human and want to stay on Earth forever! Why? You know not what you are missing.

For this reason we are preparing a sampling of the delights that await you *'above'* once you complete all you need to do to advance your soul on this plane. You can be here or there, but we will try to keep you here as much as possible while you study this material.

Let your mind unwind and let your soul take you to the stars. If you could travel over the rainbow, you would find a whole new being there that is of You—and you would delight in the glory of YOU. Why not fly over the rainbow now? The negativity of Earth surrounds you like a shroud. It causes you to doubt and feel glum whenever things are not clear or intelligible to you. On other planes there is no negativity and you *see* everything!

The world you create here on Earth is not special, but it is unique to you and your fellow residents. You all act in a panoramic play of cultures and ethics that intermingle at will in order to reenact all your fears and hopes as time evolves. One generation blends into another, but you remain as you are. You appear to be different people at different times, but you are always the same. Sometimes you are rough, and sometimes you are smoothly polished—with a façade of great intelligence, but you are always the same beneath your flesh.

When you open your eyes each morning, do you see things? What? What is it you decide to see? We can see so much more going on around you than you even pretend to know, because you choose to see only a certain area of the atmosphere and some properties of Earth. You could foreseeably (sic) see all of Earth, but most are too unsure of the human qualities you all possess to challenge any other arrangement of molecules just yet.

In the only other world you know—your dreams, you see yourself in false faces and figures of ridicule and despair, or fright and fight, but it is always *you*. You can recognize it now, yet some spend much time studying these aspects of the total personality. Few, if any, are ready to react to the content of their dreams, preferring instead to question or marvel at the information contained within them, thereby sidestepping all you know within *you* to be true about them, too.

If you could sit and watch the universe, what do you think you would find—a large world or a small *you*? You would find You, as well as a lot of others equally as advanced who are trying to reach God. You would see how difficult you make this world seem to be and why. Once you clear Earth's atmosphere, you can see it all, but many who try to advance here forget they are not truly of Earth, thus they cannot see.

You need a map of the universe now!

You need to know where you are going and why you must start your journey soon. You also need to know what to take with you and why you will need it. If your life is less than perfect now, you are on Earth. There is no way life on Earth can ever achieve harmony or peace with all that exists now. It is not the way of your world! You choose chaos and deceit as primary reasons for being out of touch with one another—and it works well to alienate all.

If you become alienated from others on Earth, it may be difficult to reestablish yourself as an integral part of the entire universe when you no longer reside here. Therefore, it is necessary that you begin now to know who you are and why you are here, in order to merge and intermingle with as many other humans as possible before leaving Earth and advancing to the next plane.

If your body thrills to music, you can feel the advancement of the vibrational atmosphere around you, but you cannot change *you*. You need total concentration to change—whether it is by nature intellectual, physical, or emotional. It is now impossible to change spiritually. As a human being, you cannot do it.

You will find yourself changing as you advance through the ages on Earth and as *you* move from one *'life'* to another, but you seldom advance beyond Earth's work. You need a change of heart and a total revamping of your ethical framework to do that, and most religions do not permit such a reestablishment of commitment. If you changed too much, you would end up ostracized by your fellows, thus most refuse to change at all.

What if you could change You—your Higher Self? Would you? No, while on Earth you are not secure enough to change anything about the real *you*. You may decide to experiment and develop other attributes, but the real *you* remains intact until another time. While tied down in this atmosphere, you cannot determine which ideals are best.

You need to fly to adjust to You!

Because you wish to keep busy, there is always something to do while on Earth, but it can keep you from doing what you came here to do. You need to contact your inner self from time-to-time to determine if you are doing your work or that of another. If you are not doing your work, you need to change immediately, but you cannot change You (the Higher Self).

The aspects of your personality highlighted on this plane are not the only ones you possess, but what you must understand while here. You may not know why you can see, smell, hear, or taste, but you need to use these senses to enlarge your life and achieve all you can; otherwise they atrophy and you become blinded or deaf in another existence in order to teach you their importance to the overall well-being of this life.

You may or may not know how to develop into the best that is *you*, but you can try. If you try and succeed, you can advance. If you try and fail, you learn enough to succeed on the next attempt. If you steadfastly refuse to try, you definitely lose the game of life.

Why refuse to try something new?
Tell us about it now...

Daily you refuse to do new things. You refuse to accept new ideas, and intelligent conversation can throw you into a whirl or give you a headache, too. Why? You do not want anything new to enter your mind while here. You like old, traditional, stale ideas rather than the new, unconventional, fresh appeal of ideas not yet conceived or developed beyond the talking stage now.

Philosophers are revered and hated by many for their insistence upon talking about why they are here and what life is or could be. Why would you care? What if they are right? Is that what bothers you about them?

When you are old and age has crippled your interest in others, you will have time to withdraw into the cocoon of your inner life. Before that time arrives, enjoy all you find wherever and whenever it may be. It is the stuff of dreams—and dreams are explorations of other aspects of *you*. You can be *you*, but need to be all you are here to be, too.

This is a difficult subject to project forward into the future of *you* due to the misconceptions of all who now choose to restrict their thoughts. You need to let your mind grow and develop every day of your life on Earth. Why is that difficult to do? You do not want to grow!

If you hate to study the ways of others, you are too ethnocentric. Ethnocentricity is not the hatred of others, rather the ignorance of all not like you. You believe '*they*' are different, but no one on Earth is different. You look alike, stand erect, feel the same emotions, and live on air and water. What are you so afraid of when you meet others? Understand your fears first—then you can shed them.

One-by-one, we intend to establish a new world order within you as you read. Let the mind go and you are *you*. Keep the mind constantly busy and it will destroy the spirit of you. Your spirit loves to be busy, but not preoccupied. You must hinder the mind's demands that keep you too busy. This is not hard to do in most circumstances. You are not too compromising within this work of art, nor having difficulty seeing into others as you look at yourself; therefore, we will begin working with you and end with *you*.

In the first era of your life on Earth you fear nothing. Once you see what all others do, you conform. Your childhood is a time when you gather much information—and never change most of it while on Earth. However, if you are to advance, you need to constantly gather wholesome and intelligent data. If restricted in doing that, your adult life will reflect it.

Once you are beyond childhood, you need to advance your sociability skills and gain greater insights into others. If you remain aloof or antisocial, you will not absorb all you need to know to advance beyond this plane, and you will be required to return until you know it. Save time and learn what you need to know now!

Join groups that reflect your interests or desires and you will get there. If you do not join groups, you have less time to enter the world's whirl of social and political functions, and it takes more time to accomplish such development. You may not like groups, but you are who determines the group. If a group is not like you, you become like the group, so be sure you are comfortable from the start when entering any group or you will lose you.

In the middle of each group is a leader. Established group or not—leaders emerge. You should try being a leader, as well as being a follower. To stay one or the other all this life is not good.

The best way to merge with another is to marry, but you do not follow this tradition any longer in good conscience. You alter such life plans at will now. Why? You do not want to merge with anyone else! You want to keep all your things for you alone. Why do that when things are not *you*? You become an automaton if you aspire to have and hold things close to you. People are necessary in your life to affirm your being. You must merge at least once in order to pass this most difficult of tests. If you do not merge with anyone while here, it is impossible to advance to the next plane.

The only one you know spiritually on Earth is *you*, but you can learn a lot about You by merging with someone else. It helps you understand what is important to *you*. If you can successfully merge, you are helped a lot when leaving this world. If you have great difficulty merging with others, you most likely will have to repeat this experience. Why? It indicates a lack of social ability! You need to know why you came to Earth before it all fits into place and you know why you are here.

If your life is over and you still do not know *you*, you cannot merge with another to cross over to the next plane. Why? You need to be unified with all aspects of your humanity while residing on Earth; therefore, many aspects of life are best handled in a common relationship, particularly if it extends beyond your generation. Your past lives on Earth explored extra-generational living and this life is based on exploring self, but you still need the entire gamut to be covered before *you* can move ahead.

At the end of this world a merger of self with others takes you all the way back to the beginning of time. If you are not ready, you will be unable to go. You need experience in every phase of this life. Thus one life is seldom enough, but it can be done. Think of all this and be sure you know why you choose not to socialize or why you do—then know what to do, otherwise your life is now incomplete.

Whatever you do, you will repeat anything you do not finish now, so get busy. Get going in whatever direction you are *not* pursuing now. If you are very social, then lend help to another who is not as social. Help them break their isolation. It will go far toward advancing *you*. If your life is lived in isolation now, seek others immediately.

If you are ill or sick at heart, you need to heal, so get into the circle of health and get well. You control all your bodily functions. Work on the world if it is no longer fit for you to use. If you decide to let it all go, you have to return. You may then have to return for more than one life, so keep working to reduce this term now.

If your life is over and you are sure you can advance, you can work to open up to the glories that will come to you in the next plane. Many are now opening to it daily. You could be one of the lucky ones, but how do you know? *You just know!*

We will partition off this work from the next segment so you can study it more deeply than one reading permits now. We have observed that you do not study as you read. You merely absorb the surface detail.

Read slowly and surely! If your mind wanders, return immediately to the spot where it went off-course. This is a form of meditation. You can meditate as you read. Be careful of your pace, because you may not have enough time to reread material, so always read slowly!

The next session is less intense and more to the point. We will be able to enjoy you more and more as you learn more and ask better questions. As teachers we are not overjoyed to have to repeat and repeat the basics, but it is necessary when there are many slow learners. We welcome all who advance rapidly, but await those who cannot.

Live each day fully until we meet again!

Chapter Two

The only one on Earth now who is related to you is *you*. If you believe You (your Higher Self) exists, you are *you* now. If you believe you do not live or work in Spirit here on Earth, you obviously have a problem.

Some do not think of Earth as a place where they are supposed to do something. They believe it is just there—and they happen to be here. If you even think you are, you are. But if you believe in some strange convoluted theory of discovery or interaction of molecules, or think you do not actually exist but in theory, you have a problem. Better start rethinking your life here immediately!

You do need time to rethink your life, but it takes less time than to rebuild it. If you built the framework of your personal belief system, you hesitate to remove any part of it; because if you remodel your original system, you may not redo it properly. Start with a well thought-out plan and practice what you preach before you mount a pulpit, otherwise you will end up in a depression one day without a clue as to why you are so down on you.

It is important to start with a positive attitude, because if all goes bad you do not have as far to go to get back to *home base*. We speak of Earth as *home base*, meaning it is where you are now. It is definitely not the only place to be in the universe, nor is it the only place you dwell even now, but it is the only fully-awake place you know at this time, thus it has to be maintained as your *home base* when you travel to other places.

To travel in the dark is the most difficult way to find your way in life, but it is great to go into the dark and exclude all light in order to appreciate the dawn. The dawn of anyone's life is when that person sees the light for the first time, but may not realize it until later. Why? Because one can be dazzled by the light.

To know God is within *you* is not a big deal, but some of you are so out-of-touch with reality in your minds that you believe there is no God. What a relief if you find out there is a god? Not at all! It produces the greatest confusion such souls can feel while here. If you have always believed, it is hard to fathom how awful God is, but imagine those who never realized it and suddenly are confronted with the immensity of it all. You cannot imagine the stunning sensation to the mind of a non-believer when they realize God is this and all that exists!

The World of Tomorrow is not here today, but being built daily as it appears. If you do not live now, your tomorrow is one of frustrated ambitions and hopelessness. If you live fully each day, you will know you are *you*.

The only one to subsist on Earth is the one who is not of Earth. You will hear more on that later, but for now it is enough to realize you live and breathe in an atmosphere that is inadequate for all of you to survive in much longer. Some who live and breathe on Earth have no difficulty due to following other directions of activity. They, too, are of Earth—but not human or animal. Wait for the day to come when we can sit together and talk of such things, until then, now is the time to realize you have much you need to absorb and know here on Earth before you can move into your future.

If your life here on Earth excludes You (the Higher Self), you will not grow. You have to find your niche, then circulate and announce what it is. Once everyone knows you are *you*, the whole being is prosperous once again.

If you do not feel at home, you are not!

What if you were to grow and develop into another human being? Would you still be you? No, you would have to select another aspect of *you* to enter that life contract. It would take that aspect an entire lifetime to work on that life before you would know what happened, unless you elected to guide that aspect—then *you* would know!

Why are you upset if you are not in charge? You fear others can change you—which is ridiculous! You cannot change anyone, nor can any other being change you—nor can another aspect of *you* be changed by you.

What about *you*? It sounds alive and breathing, but is it human? You know now that things are not what they appear to be here, but you still believe *you* are as you are. That is why we are here! We are helping you shed years of misguided information you received from those unable to understand why you are you or why you cannot be someone else.

The only entity in creation powerful enough to enter You is God. God alone is of such great magnitude that you could be changed in an instant, but it seems a bit egotistical to believe you would be singled out for such a treat. Does it not?

Why try to be someone else? Why act a part? Why not live as you are? Because you enjoy being several different people—and believe if you have personality splits of any depth it enlarges your experience here. It is not advisable to do this, because you could end up splitting into several personalities at will.

The split of one human into two is impossible, but the mind can shatter. It can be put back together again and again, even create several different people, but not in the way a body is put back together. It requires the advancement of the ego and a few other things, but it can be done.

By the time you finish this book, you may know several different people who remind you of the seven different personality traits we describe along the way, but you will not know seven people with split personalities. Why? The glue that holds us all together is not of ego, but of spirit. The spirit of anyone is not viewable by you—only by God.

Before you can split, you ask for permission to do so and may or may not be granted such permission. It is your design, but it has to be approved. If all of *you* insists upon the change, you can be altered. Initially it is left up to *you*, but it can be vetoed by those above *you* who are more cognizant of your growth and will not let you do anything here to derail *you*.

Whenever you fear anyone, you let others enter your mind. They cannot enter *you*, but you give them access to your mind, where they can fully absorb your being. You gave them the power—not someone else, so you are being taken over with your permission—not someone else trying to enter you. We constantly repeat this because of false information abroad today that states some people can be *'taken over'* while meditating—which would be laughable if not such a serious problem now.

When you fear anything, you give it power!

If you fear a man or woman, you give that one the opportunity to overrule your mind—and usually you lose! You cannot expect others to adopt your changes of attitude in order to know you, but you can expect them to misinterpret you to all. Why be naïve? It is easier to follow than to assume responsibility for yourself.

What if your life on Earth became so terrifying you could not live here another moment? You might think about suicide, but instead might let yourself be murdered. You might even tempt others to harm or rape you, but it is you projecting onto others your fear that makes such people aggress against you. This is absolutely true!

What if you decide you have not lived enough? You would begin to take others' lives and confiscate their goods or family, but you could not get to their souls. They cannot be attacked or given over to you, only what they are willing to share.

If you attack, you may lose or you may win, but your life is diminished by it. You lose the energy needed to aggress against others. This defeat is of self and causes anger to manifest within every aspect of your life—and ends with you becoming ill.

Illness is so often caused by aggression that anger can be listed as a major cause; but if you state that to an angry individual, they will turn on you and aggress toward you—even if you are their physician. Doctors seldom attack the cause of an illness, because it is too sensitive to discuss an individual's problems of behavior when not trained in the area of psychodynamics, but it truly is the root of most ailments. When will all medical types begin to do the really tough work? Only when amateurs and frauds relieve them of much money.

We will not let anyone doing God's work enter into the work of those who conspire to defeat individuals—and this includes the world of medicine. If you cannot find a drug in stores, you can easily grow it—but do you know what to do with it? No, and you do not attempt to learn—in order to blame others for your pain.

By refusing to accept responsibility, you can ignore the cause of discontent originating within you. You do not have to acknowledge that some of your life choices were bad—or far from good. You do not have to argue or concentrate on your thinking processes that confirm your bad behavior being rooted in evil doing.

If you gossip, you have done evil so many ways that it is assumed gossip is always negative. However, if your conversation is intended to promote another's best interests, it is not called gossip. In fact, today it is thought to be suspicious behavior if you talk positively a lot about others. Even the person most likely to benefit will suspect you have an ulterior motive for spreading positive messages about them.

What on Earth is going on now to cause such mistrust? You are all afraid others are beating you to the prize! What prize? The future! You are afraid others will be there before you are. So what if they are? If it is their future, too, how does that affect you? It does not. Think of you and your future and you find yours will satisfy no one else but you. Therein is the future—not over there somewhere!

For the short time you are on Earth, why not build a great life here and now? After a number of lifetimes in which you worked hard and life was difficult, you get lazy. You do not gain anything easily, because if you did, you would not have come to Earth to learn how to work now!

You came to Earth to study such things as negativity and its impact on a positive being of light, or how to exist in a world of materialistic aspects when you are a spiritual concept. The idea that you are a concept does not sit well with many—why? Because ego tells you to become all you are and all you can be—not to become spiritual, the one thing you already are.

The ego is the basis of all evil in this world!

You are not evil, but your ego can concentrate its energy on you and yours and command such a tremendous amount of effort that you cannot fight it off. If your ego is not working for you, then why do you have one? To protect you in this atmosphere from what could kill you physically. You need to know all there is to know about the world in which you live, but that knowledge can take you into areas far removed from God. In any area where ego reigns supreme, man is not likely to start honoring God.

In *The World of Today* you have many things going for you, but you seldom notice. Why? You are so absorbed in the future, you ignore today!

If you only live now, why do you believe tomorrow will arrive? You have faith. You believe. However, if someone asks you if you believe in God you may not readily agree that you do. Why? Either you are not serious or you wish to appear to be different. You may want the attention it brings by saying you do not believe in God—but you still believe. If you do not believe, you are stricken with grief or fear of death. It never occurs to those who say they are agnostics that they have to believe in order to say God does not or probably does not exist. It is silly to argue about it, God is!

If you live now and believe only in today, why not be available tomorrow? Of course, it sounds silly! You sound silly whenever you debate issues that are settled—and even been dramatically proven. Why waste a life on such silliness? You want attention!

So much time is now spent trying to make everyone look important—and it cannot be. You are not important. You live. You exist. You will be, but you are no different than billions-upon-billions of others. Why protest so much? Ego!

The ego is not apparent in any beings other than humans, but it exists elsewhere. In the lower plane they prepare you for this one by introducing ego, but it is nothing like the madness now experienced in this world here on Earth. Earth is the work of God, but this world is man's creation—and a sorry one now.

Why do you all have to harm one another to get ahead? You want what your neighbors have! You want money more than love. You want independence without the act of becoming free. You want what others work for, and then destroy it. If you do such things, your life is not thriving now.

What to do to get Earth back to where it was before the world took this wrong path? You have to go back! Once you decide to correct your work, you will force all others to change, too. It is a chain reaction! Only one needs to change to force an entire string of people to change as well. If you object to unfair treatment of others, you may influence some; but if you do not treat others unfairly, you set a precedent. That precedent is then followed and accepted, even if you are not.

You wish to be popular,
But if you lead—you never are!

All of your leaders now are unstable due to the vocalness (sic) of your negativity. You truly believe leaders need to be torn down and replaced every few years. Why? Why not let them tear down their work instead? You hate to have anyone above you. For the same reason you hate to report to God. You would prefer to stumble over yourself now rather than go to church and worship.

You do not like the clergy. Why? They are leaders and believe in God. You relish any dispute among the clergy or any evil-doers among them, while doing worse. Why do you hate those who are no less human than you? You are jealous!

People who know nothing of work are seldom impressed by the hard work of others. You know who you are. We do not point out such obvious displays of laziness, because you know who you are, but we will point out jealousy. Jealousy is obvious only once it is discovered. It is like leprosy. It is not noticeable until it is too far advanced to be easily cured.

If you deny you like something you actually love, you are jealous. You are jealous if you continually deny another has made a point or is in the right when they obviously proved it. You are jealous if you decide beforehand something is wrong merely because another said it is good or right. Jealousy in its strongest form is when you see another do the right thing and refuse to follow their lead.

To refuse to follow in the evil ways of others is most appropriate, but how many times since adolescence have you been led into such areas of misbehavior? If this is true more than *seldom* or *never,* you are in dangerous company now. Most will not be tormented by evil-doers once they commit their lives to God.

It is no fun to torment in every way someone better than you, but it is done. Why? Jealousy is a vicious attack of the conscience that can equal death of the soul. It can be so violent that it kills. It can be so nasty that it destroys reputations of virtuous people. It can be so evil that it persuades good people to depart from the paths of other good people and persuade them to be bad.

When was the last time you went out of your way to help a stranger? If you say it is dangerous to help people you do not know, you can never say you help others. Most people in need are not easy to immediately recognize. They created situations and you are there to interact with them to establish some degree of negativity vs. positive outcome. It is they who know not you—not the reverse. You fail if you do not pass this test.

Why are you tested? In order to see if virtue works for you or not. Virtue does its job—or not. Virtue is not a trait of character. It just is! If you are a virtuous person you help all accosted by others in a virulent manner. If you are not, you join the attackers. Is that easy enough to understand?

Virtue is less obvious in a crowd, but is still there. If only one virtuous person stands up and attacks aggressors, most people side with virtue. If no one stands up in such instances, all lack virtue. They are not virtuous people, but this is how to change that:

Sit in a chair and talk aloud to the wall. Tell the wall how tired, angry, upset, indifferent to others, etc. you are and then listen to the wall. Do you hear anything?

If you hear something, you are in contact with your Spiritual Guides. If you hear nothing, listen more closely to detect a murmur or sound. Only you can silence your ego long enough to hear your spiritual self awaken.

What if you do not have Spiritual Guides?

That is not possible! No one comes to Earth alone—without anyone to direct or help them. No one's Spiritual Guides abandon them. They may wish to leave, but such Guides cannot. Their lives are entailed within the life of the human being they are here to guide. They, too, are judged at the end of this life for how well their human charge lived now. It behooves your Guide to keep in constant contact with you, but how is that possible if your ego is always in total control and denies you have a Spiritual Guide?

Listen! Do not sit and stare into space—listen. Hear the voice within you speak of YOU and your dreams. Listen to why you are here. Talk aloud, speak to that voice and hear it return your words—and listen! If you need help learning how to listen to your inner wisdom, let us introduce you to the art of meditation. To get started...

Sit in a comfortable position and stretch your spine to its fullest extent. Breathe deeply and ask for peace.

Once you feel peace caused by your spirit circulating through you, exhale deeply to clear your lungs of stale air...then inhale peace and exhale negativity—over and over again.

As you breathe, count inhalations up to four and then back to one— over and over again. When you successfully accomplish this, you are meditating!

There are many who meditate, but few who are ready to change their lives as a direct result of information gleaned during or following their meditations. Why? They do not believe in God. Yes, you can meditate and not believe in God. They are not synonymous. You are not a believer if you try everything—or maintain meditation is just another pleasurable way to spend time.

If you cannot take enough time to study the effects of meditation on your life, you are not considered to be a student of ours. If you do not meditate, you cannot answer questions articulated by your Higher Self, nor can you hear answers from all who constitute this higher wisdom. You cannot believe in God if you cannot hear the words of wisdom and know God is.

After experimenting with the above meditation, perhaps stewing about it for a while, you are ready to try another meditative exercise.

Sit on a tall, straight-backed chair and lean your head back until it touches the chair. Clench your hands into fists—then relax them. Do this for several minutes.

Now sit still for several minutes. Let your mind slow down and imagine you are being lifted off the chair—as though flying to another place and time.

If you can visualize such a flight, you are meditating—and doing quite well! If you cannot do this, plan to fly away from this world and seek peace of mind another day. The world has become too much for you to handle right now.

The only way to be you is to enjoy yourself as much as possible. If you do that, your life will reflect your happiness. We enjoy working with all who find our work important. We do not waste any effort on those disinterested in working with us. Why would you be any different? You all have egos that insist everyone must think as you do, but no one does, so do not waste energy trying to convert others!

It is not you who needs God. It is God within *you* that needs to be bigger than your ego and insists you, too, must let others be themselves in order to find God within in their own way and their own time. Be aware, if you force others to be of God, you are not of God!

In many ways the course of this book is a winding one, but it will cover all the points of interest you need to study along the way. Enjoy yourself today!

Chapter Three

The only one who knows more than you about *you* is your superior(s) above this plane. Some of you act as if you are superior beings— even believe you are superior to your fellow man, which is very humorous to all of us above you. You cannot enjoy the afterglow of life while on Earth, nor can you see it, but it exists. Why not put your life in perspective and enjoy this time on Earth, rather than take yourself too seriously?

This is a time when much change is imminent on Earth and people are not prepared for it, but anticipate it with delight. Why? Why do you relish change—especially if it could mean the end of all you know now? You are aware Earth is no longer hospitable to man. You realize you could do better in another atmosphere. Yet you fear nothing now.

Pity the poor, frightened beings who know nothing of God or man and wish to stay on Earth as is. The world is changing into a short-term investment where all exchange currency daily. No one is content. No one believes the good times of today will last. No one believes tomorrow will be better.

All seek retaliation for wrong doing, then overturn it. Why? To be in the wrong is not difficult to understand, but to let others determine the final outcome of another's life hits too hard at the core of man's worry about this life. You fear this life is not yours. You feel it is not going well and may end before you are ready. This is a false belief. Life ends on Earth only when *you* decide to end it.

What if you decide to enter a race and then change your mind about running in it? What if you decide to begin a new job and then sell out? (To sell out refers to not doing your work while on assignment.) What if you decide to marry someone and turn away from them at the altar during the ceremony? What if you adopt a child and return it? These are all major decisions that end badly due to previously inadequate thinking. Your life on Earth is not that ill-considered! You are here for a purpose and will stay here until it is accomplished—or you ask for a replacement to take over for you.

Why bother coming to Earth?

You are here to learn something on a spiritual level that is crucial to your total field of endeavor, and you either learn it now or continually return until you do. Your life on Earth is not the same as what you had elsewhere or even here at another time, but is the same as lives you are experiencing now on different phases of this plane.

Your Spiritual Guides reside on this plane in order to be of assistance to you. Angels are much higher—not higher in importance, but on a higher plane. You are not privy to all the steps and procedures needed to advance beyond this plane, because you are not going anywhere until you finish this life.

Why not work at this work, and if you care to develop it further, learn more then? To work at spiritual work during the years devoted to this world's work will end in an endless stream of energy going up to the next plane without a firm foundation established on this one. If you practice rising to a higher level, you need to be able to return to this plane at any time, thus you must establish a firm foundation here or be lost in space.

Whatever you need, you get. If you need a new coat and hat, it is there for you. It may not be fashionable or what you would have bought or made, but you get one. If you want something more than what is provided by the universe for your use, you must go after it and obtain it yourself—not take what another earned or needs.

Gluttony is the act of eating beyond the body's capacity to feed itself properly. It results in fat. If you are grossly overweight, you are greedy. You are out to feed on all you can find, because you do not want to wait until you are hungry, or you fear food will not be there when you need it. You need not fret. The world is unable to prevent a hard worker from obtaining food.

If you try to work and it is denied, or you are paid nothing for doing it, you have the right to complain and walk away. However, it is correct to not get paid for work not done. You need to do your work and should be paid for whatever you hire out to do, but God pays best.

No one else in this life can supply your needs better than *you*— except God. God is obviously not another person, even though some people are treated as if they are gods. First, finish your work and then see how fast its worth is noticed. If you are not given your fair share, move.

Why are people now moving to other areas all over the globe? Food is the reason given, but it is often caused by greed. Most who move believe they can get more somewhere else. Some even leave their families behind for more money. Why? They fear being left behind. They want credit for work not done. They have not cleared the initial work of this plane.

This plane does not consist of only one level. Many levels make up one plane. Development is accentuated by the degree of intensity each person enters work of the next level of a plane. This sounds mysterious, definitely archaic to you, but clear to us. You need to develop before you can advance, so you climb one step at a time, or one lifetime at a time, or one segment of a life at a time, before you reach the top of a plane and can advance to the next one.

If your world is not of Today, how can it become Tomorrow? You cannot answer, but we can. You need to know how to live in the present to the exclusion of the past and future, yet all seek predictions to prove you are on the right path. Predictions are just that! They cannot be proven until they occur. So many factors occur in each life to hinder the progress of even one prediction about a person's destiny that no one can predict if a child will end up ready to be with God or not.

You are not asked to predict your life's end, but you will know it in time to order your next life. You will know it before you leave this plane. What if you knew all you would do in this life before living it? Would you want to do it? No, you know many areas of your life now and can make them happen immediately, but refuse to do all that is necessary to make it all come true now. Why? You are stubborn, ignorant of God's plan, and unable to believe in *you*—or you are doing only what comes into your path and not looking to do more.

While on Earth, no one is close to erasing their slate. For example, no one here will ascend directly to the plane where angels dwell, but there are people preaching such nonsense now—and fools who believe them. You work your way up—step-by-step, only then can you do all that is required.

One of the best things you can do for *you* while on Earth is to sit and meditate, then dream of life as it is and as it should be. If you can change your dreams within or during meditation, it is! If you cannot change anything then, you at least did something constructive with your life.

Among the few people able to dwell in the rarified atmosphere of the higher planes are those who can enter it at will—and such exertion demonstrates their obedience to God. Few people are centered within themselves enough to exert pressure on their will; therefore, the likelihood of anyone doing that in this time and space is highly suspicious to us and requires a visitation. We do visit!

If you ever meditated and felt you had a long nap or left the room, you did. It is not that hard to meditate so deeply that you cannot sense what you did then. If your hands are loose and relaxed, it is harder to leave your seat, but if you clench your hands on the arms of a chair, you may easily lift your body and move about while your mind and spirit remain rooted in meditation. It is no big deal! What if you do rise? What if you do see yourself? What if you cannot feel anything? What if your body lost all feeling, and you can see yourself as if from a long distance? You are still you and alive in this time.

You may have any number of strange experiences as you meditate, but they are not as strange as you are to us. You have to develop an interest in being all you can be before experimenting to discover how much you know about the body's various abilities you can manipulate and use. Once you learn, you can use your body up to all its limits.

The body is the easiest to study of the three—body, mind and spirit, so what happens next? Learning to use your mind! The mind is not like the body, but is definitely knowable—compared to Spirit. You will never know the spiritual nature of man until you are no longer in flesh. You may learn significant details while here, but never the entire story—that must wait until you fully return to Spirit at the end of this life.

If you could leap forward in time, would you? No, you would be too afraid. You can enter meditation at any time of the day, but do not. Why? You do not wish to engage in anything that reduces your attention to ego matters.

The ego is rooted in this world and time frame, but it can be tamed enough to let you reserve short periods of time in which to exit far enough to meditate—then it exerts its power over you once again. If you leapt forward, the ego would be helpless. The ego's stance is: *It does not need you. It just is!* But the ego is not *you*, nor does it exist beyond this life. You will continue on in Spirit, but the ego is shed along with the body when you die—that is why it complains and fears death.

In the annals of time are a few who leapt to their deaths only to be returned to Earth—but few, if any, of those returned were dead. If you believe in life-after-death experiences, and most of you do, you can see why this is the basis of reincarnation discussions all over the globe. Why? Why would you believe in a *'near death'* experience and not believe you are eternal by nature? Does not compute!

The only time to be on Earth is when you are more or less compelled to learn to use negative energy, or to dwell among those you angered by evil doings, or you are trying to amass credit for another assignment elsewhere. However, some try to return because they simply became totally convinced that life is found only on Earth and they cannot let go of it. You will program your mind now to accept that life goes on and will take you to higher vistas, thus there should be fewer and fewer '*lost souls'* wandering outside the perimeter of your plane.

What if you came to a crossroads and a car coming toward you refused to stop? Would you beam a bright light, beep your horn, or let him go? All three are wise choices, but the last one saves you. This is the choice of all who watch loved ones fighting to stay on Earth in order to help those who will be left behind. Give them light, talk to them, but let them go. Encourage them to go! Sit and talk of the time when you will be together again. Even in what you call a '*coma'* people can hear and cogitate, so do not let this time go to waste. Help whomever you can to cross over, and you will receive a blessing from God.

Within the door of the future remains a shadow of today, but yesterday never reaches that far. You will remain in the doorway only as long as it takes to cross over. Once on the other side, you are there. If you arrive at the door and do not wish to cross over, you may return, because you are not dead. You cannot die and cross over, then return to Earth.

If you hear of a '*near death'* experience, recognize the person who had the episode was not dead, but alive and well and able to repeat what was seen. These scenes are repeated and exaggerated over time until all who have similar episodes agree they are the same, but they are not alike, because no two people are alike spiritually. The egos of some people are much alike, but never their Spirit.

What happens when a person goes beyond the normal opening and views the ending as being similar to a tunnel? It is not death. It is the rapid projection of Spirit into the next area surrounding your plane, and it is here that Spirit rests until admittance is granted. You are not asked to enter—and you may or may not be given entrance. Some elderly folks pray daily for admittance, but do not receive it until all their earthly chores are done, while others go quickly. *It is never the same!*

Where you are is not important, but what you are is important! Who you know does not concern anyone outside *you*, so it is unworthy of you to struggle to know others when you cannot identify yourself and your needs. While on Earth what you do daily is your job. If you do not understand that all you do is all you are, you will return again and again. If you can grasp this single thread of wisdom now, you can immediately drop this class.

We will not bother you now with the details of future travel or with old-fashioned homilies on how to live. You know how to live! What you do not know is how to enjoy *you* and your life while on Earth. Once you do, then it is time to move forward into the future. Until then, we will work on you as is.

Work out a pattern of peaceful coexistence and you have the framework set for your future life. Gain empathy for others' feelings and you are ready to experience life in another galaxy. Give of yourself and you will gain more than you give, but selfishly prevent others from gain and you will lose. Work is not a life in itself, but a life gains as it does its job.

Whatever you see or say
Becomes another view of you!

If you do not answer your life's *call*, you will not find it later. If you have too many interests and cannot do all of them, a splinter of *you* will enter an activity and pursue it until that energy is extinguished and can be returned to the central being of *you*. If you doubt this, remember the case of the jealous man who would not let his wife divorce him, because he no longer loved her and was afraid someone else did. Why would he care? You just do! You care and pursue that life course of staying married versus getting a divorce until somewhere along life's path your two 'lives' rejoin the central being and become less and less powerful, thus all of *you* can reunite and be stronger for dual experiences.

Whatever you do, remember it is not about *you*. The life episode in which you are part of that entity continues and helps *you* develop. You are not splitting or dividing—rather separating slightly in order to reunite and knit a stronger string of events that represent this life.

Work on the extreme aspects of life and you become less and less conservative—and you learn to tolerate the more conservative among you. Remain conservative always and you learn very little.

Wherever you go, you find others are already there or they just left. To ignore their input or suggest they are unwise is to admit you are a fool, too. Be of good cheer when you meet fellow human beings. You are the only humans in the universe, so enjoy the distinction. You are not the supreme beings you may wish to believe you are, but you are.

We will end this session now with this thought: Work is not work if you do what you think needs to be done, or you wish to do it. Work is not work if you love what you are doing. You will love whatever, if you work at anything long enough to produce a great product.

Remember the way to work is: Do not sit and stare at what needs to be done. Instead, enjoy the moment and do whatever you can. We work and will return in a bigger vehicle in the future.

Chapter **Four**

The World of Tomorrow sounds like a Disney ride, but it is not. It is the ride of your life, and where it takes you is not home but away from it. If you cannot imagine living anywhere else but where you live now, you cannot imagine the future of *you*. You should try to imagine *you* as you will be, and if you cannot, you have the wrong book in hand now.

The World of Today is less and less solid as you look at it, because tomorrow is encroaching upon it. Once tomorrow is here, today disappears. If you watch the sun set, it moves slowly toward the horizon, but quickly slips down the last few inches—or so it appears. If you watch the sun rise, it arrives much slower by comparison. Why? You anticipate it so much that it takes longer to create a vision than to acknowledge the end is here.

While man goes about his business and woman does hers, each is content that the other knows who each is—right? Not anymore! All are confused now and mixed up about roles and sexes, as well as every aspect known to mankind. Why? Because the end is coming faster than anticipated and many have not had any opportunity to experience all these other paths and need/want to do so before they leave Earth forever.

You think you never asked to be born, but you did. You asked for birth and a family to support you in your venture—helping or hindering you as you deserved. This decision to go forward and live on Earth is not the same as deciding to die—but close. You have to decide why you are here before you can decide to leave—either way, it is your decision.

Within a life are several different people who come to you and leave you, but some remain with you always. Why? You want them to be there for you, and you will do whatever it takes to make sure it happens. You may choose them as parents, siblings, or other relatives, but you may also marry them—it happens!

There are some who talk constantly about 'soul mates' as though there is only one other individual in the entire world who can be their lover or mate. Nonsense! The world is not a solid mass, nor is it consistent. How could you find only one person to meet all your needs? Not easily! You would have to spend your entire life searching, and then settle for the best of whatever you sampled. Not as bad as never looking and instead marrying the first person you set eyes on, but not much better, either.

You cannot expect anyone else to meet all your needs, because they are *your* needs—not someone else's needs. If you think another has something you want, you may be envious or wise, but it is your decision whether or not you do something about it. To marry in order to obtain what you do not have is a very foolish course to take, but one which is most often followed.

You should observe the other person carefully and decide if you will be content or not with that individual. If not, fully explore another before you run to yet another. Each person has unique feelings and aspirations which may in the long run help you be *you*—or not.

Realize the end is:
The beginning of another you!

Be careful with the life you live on Earth or you may ruin your chances to advance. Why would you risk a bad marriage? To advance your real reasons for coming to Earth!

You must earn a living—one way or another, get along with all others, and do no evil to anyone. Marriage provides the framework for all three necessary tasks to be accomplished and done well, but it can also be a trap into which you fall and never leave.

To do evil is easier in a marriage than in any other relationship. You may not love the other or vice versa, which sets up a situation where one or the other betrays the trust of the mate and establishes a lifelong condition in which both are at odds or hate-filled. One may hate the other and decide to divorce—and evil can be perpetrated. It only takes two people to create a climate of hate, ugliness, and ultimate divorce; but it takes only two people to create an Eden, too.

Why not use your hands and work on a project that will aid you in becoming the best you can be? You can design something to fit the needs of others or you can do it for yourself. If you are a designer, you usually let others do the actual work and thus lose a sense of accomplishment; but if you design and implement the plan, you believe all the work is yours. Let your love shine in whatever you do!

What about when you are not *you*? Do you always feel like yourself now? Do you ever feel like someone is trying to change you? If so, it is *you* trying to correct something wrong within you then. *You* is the only one who can change you—no one on Earth can.

Why would anyone want to change you? You certainly try to change others every day, so it is natural they will try to change you, too. We would recommend you stay away from anyone who believes very differently from you until such time as you are solidly grounded in your beliefs—otherwise you run the risk of losing your beliefs or having them diluted. Much of what you know is fluid and changeable, so you can change thoughts easily without adopting new principles.

The only time your world Today reaches Tomorrow is when you cross over at the end of this life—but then it is too late if you need to change. Why wait until Tomorrow to be you and live accordingly? Live now like it is tomorrow, because it is the best course of action you can take today.

How to live in The World of Tomorrow enters the mind first, then seeps into your spirit—and if accepted, enters the body. Meanwhile, you do not actually leave Today. You need others to explore the days of your future if you wish to document it, but you often go it alone just for fun.

How do you do that? You dream! If you dream and remember nothing, you intentionally wipe it out. Why do that? Because you do not want to remember or be persuaded into doing something that leads you to change.

Change of mind, style, and life is required if you wish to live tomorrow as well as you live today, but most believe it can be done without making any adjustments. This is where the life of one person differs from the rest: One prepares and exaggerates the need to change now, while another steadfastly remains rooted in today—or even worse, yesterday.

If you enjoy reenacting the past, you must realize you are losing today while doing it. You say it is only a little recreation designed to delve into the past in various ways, but it all takes away from today. If you do not live now, your future is diminished!

You need to prepare for Tomorrow now, but do not attempt to enter it just yet. You need to make preparations to begin the process, but do not need to finish them. All of this life is necessary preparation for the next plane, because this is the final realm of this section of development.

Various planes make up different sections of your life as a total soul. Your life here is not as deep or shallow as one of the planes within this section, but it culminates in a grand exploration of the physical world. You need to master negativity and how to manipulate mass, otherwise the work is the same as on other planes within this section.

You will never know who is going to be your father or mother until ready to be born unto Earth. Why? You do not need a mother or father until then, and it is only to get you started—not for all your life. You may not know if you can do something until asked to do it, and even then you may not be aware of what you can do.

Coming to live on Earth is not like that. You know when you are ready, because you asked to be here. You asked for specific parents who might be able to help or hinder your progress in attaining a particular level of development. It then becomes your life and you live it!

What if you lived on Earth with a family you did not want or were not born into? You would be responsive to the needs of the one who established the birth, but others are always considered to be possible parents, too. You may start with one family and end within several others in order to establish several different lifestyles in just one life.

No relationship structure is established without the knowledge of how it may change as time goes on. You may have young parents or choose old ones, but you know from the beginning that things will change. You accepted that challenge! Sometimes you actually seek an unstable set of parents in order to *'preordain'* your certain growth due to their growth—or not of spirit. You always choose! You lose or not, depending upon your willingness to change.

Now that you know why you came to Earth, or rather who you chose to be with to start your journey, you will begin noticing signposts along the way. Was early life easy or hard? Were you loved or ignored? Were you hostile or loving toward your family? These questions require hard answers—and those answers lead to the major decision of your life.

Why stay as you are?
Why not become all you can be?

The answer is: *Neither you nor the soul within you is ready for drastic changes now.* You need to alter one area at a time or you will require major surgery to repair the damage. If you try for immediate change, you may end up in the psychiatric ward of your local hospital, rather than become enlightened. However, if you never try to change, you will die and have to return to this work. Either way—you lose, so be careful in your selections and permit yourself to advance in a slow, methodical, rational manner, or at least make only one change at a time.

We know of instances where people decide to rid themselves of all family responsibilities before their time. They then spend their entire existence and life on Earth trying to beat the clock. You cannot cheat the soul!

You must do whatever needs to be done to advance your spiritually or pay the price in other ways. Simply stated, ethics is a manner of putting priorities in place that establish the greatest amount of good for the greatest number of people residing within a particular society. However, such ethics must change as the society changes, otherwise the rules break down and chaos ensues.

You are not the only one here who is upset by Earth's changes, but some are extremely morbid and even dangerous to themselves due to fear of death. We would caution you to be careful of any who are unsure of who they are, since they may decide to end their lives on Earth prematurely.

What is it about fear of death that so many cling to it now? It is not sane or safe to fear death, but most of you have at one time or another. Even now—you may fear death. Why? Because you fear change!

Change is why you came to Earth!

If you had chosen to remain the same or similar to whatever you were, you would not have arrived here. This is a totally different environment from all other planes and sections. It differs so much that few wish to enter it for more than a very short time, which is why some do not live long or commit suicide when very young. It is not an ideal environment for very spiritual beings, but very necessary for them to develop beyond their own limitations.

You will never be asked to kill yourself. You were told to never commit suicide, and you are asked to not end your life intentionally by flaunting your safety in dangerous situations and places. Otherwise, you may order this life to end. It is your choice!

You may decide to end your life seven years from now (one life cycle later) or you may decide to end it in less time, but it is your decision. Usually the life cycle ends in spring or fall—seldom in summer or winter. Why? You do not physically change as much during those seasons. Remember, change can kill you!

What if you changed so much you could not recognize yourself? You would have an identity crisis! It happens all the time during the life of anyone who refuses to know who they really are. You may already be such a person or you may decide to become someone else due to jealousy or envy of others.

Do not try to change you! Let God do it for you. You can pray and meditate until all is changed, or you can experiment and answer all the signs presented along the way that indicate change is needed. Regardless, each way is the same.

The only one you can fully trust to know *you* is God within You. *You* cannot trust you here, because ego is such a strong monitor of self-interest that it can persuade you to do silly, nonsensical things designed to promote self-interest—which in the end will not succeed.

Life is not all you seek. You seek happiness. You seek success. You seek wealth. You may even seek health. But they are all given when you are *you*!

We listen as our scribe counsels lost souls and needlessly worried men and women about their lives, and we learn much about life on Earth. Do you ever *really* listen to what bothers others? Do you care? If not, you will have to learn their lessons!

Your life is not the only life on Earth most of you have had, but the only one you can live now. It does not matter if you were here ten or twelve times, or if you had a lot of big titles, great responsibilities, or helped mold the modern world. What matters is that you learned skills needed in this life to overcome present difficulties.

We will use *The Scribe* as an example. She came to Earth as an Egyptian of longstanding who lived there several lives—and was a scribe each time. In those times scribes painted symbols rather than writing out texts. Today she is learning to draw stories for people in graphic ways. She depicts the life of those who call upon her to do so. She never willingly sought this art. It is a gift from those who reward her diligence to this work now.

You may wonder about things you do well, and wonder why others cannot do them nearly as well. Do not worry any longer. You had lots of practice in other lives or you could not do it well now. All skill requires much practice!

If your life here is to be repeated, and most of you act like it is, then you should learn as many different skills as possible now that will enable you to have an easier life the next time. If you think this is your last time on Earth, study to make sure you learn all you can from this experience. If you do not work now, you will have wasted this time on Earth.

Tomorrow is based on today, and today is now! So let us begin seeing ourselves as we are today and visualize how we will be tomorrow—then let it all go. It will then happen as you see it now!

For you, this is a difficult life simply because it is the life you have now. In the past you also had difficult lives and survived, having learned from them or not, but you are here now. Live to be alive and live as long as you remain on Earth!

Do not seek refuge in another person or begin to hate those in power. Be you at all times and you will have all the power you need. Power is the ability to control you—not control others—and to live as you wish.

This is the end of a discussion about why you are unable to change others—which changed you! Why? You are now ready to change.

When ready for anything, it happens! Be ready for love, and you fall in love. Be ready for success, and it is yours. Be ready for God, and you are.

We wish all who study with us could comprehend messages not written in black and white, but we will settle for this—if it is all you can understand now. We agree to help you persuade others you come in contact with to permit you to enjoy all you learn at this time. If you are so confined to this atmosphere that you cannot move away from the keepers of your body, we suggest you meditate and escape this reality for short periods of time. This refreshes your spirit and enables us to teach you even more.

Please reread this chapter before you go any further.

Chapter Five

The only world to be in is here and now. You need to keep your hands and feet here, but let the mind travel elsewhere. If you feel it is too far out, retract it to this place and time. Begin immediately to see the world is you and *you* are the world, even if it seems to be so big and marvelous you cannot believe it could all be YOU—it is!

Earth is a smallish planet that revolves around your sun without anyone being the wiser in universes several galaxies and forty-five light years away. You might believe *the universe* covers all things, but it is a term used when describing you and your world—not God's work. The universe is a concept so small that it limits your comprehension of God and the work of God. Think big—then enlarge it to comprehend how large it is, then double, triple, quadruple, etc. until you tire of doing it and you still have no comprehension of God's work or YOU!

In this world are many who dream, but few who act upon their dreams. Why? If you follow your dreams and see where they take you, you can do much and gain many friends, but few will emulate you. Why? They cannot change.

Change is how this world came to be and how it will end, but few are willing to acknowledge their part in it. Why? It is hard to distinguish between that which is right and that which is might.

If you believe in yourself, from time-to-time you will see you have to sit back and review your history to determine if you did all you wished to do, as well as why you continue to do what you do now. If you decide it is of no use to pursue the same course, steer your life in another direction or go into the inner self and explore where it differs from your original plan.

If you plan to go forward, you need a map, otherwise you will never leave; if you do, you may not find You (the Higher Self). You sometimes lose yourself, then try to figure out why you did whatever. It is all done to educate you in the work of God.

You cannot remain as is forever or *you* will become so stagnant you cannot live in this water. The air and water circulate for a reason. They grow stale and stagnate when they need more oxygen. You require oxygen, too. It is the main ingredient in everything you do and are, so be sure you know how to extract the maximum from your atmosphere or die here helplessly.

The hope of all people now is to be successful and never have to work. *"What an agreeable thought,"* you say. We think it is not at all a good way to idealize. Instead, look at you as is and see all you could have done so far if you had only known God was working within *you*, in order to help you prepare the way for others to advance here.

Would you feel confident that the time to work is when you are young or would you wonder: *"Why do I wait?"* The need to wait until others are also ready is human—not at all like any other being in the universe. Most adults in your world are unwilling to admit their work is the most interesting facet of their lives. Some will and they will be criticized for saying it. Why? It is the dream of all to be idle now. You think idleness is the way of the world today—and you are the only one working at menial pursuits. You need to awaken to these times.

You need to pursue dreams,
And be you at all times!

The only one you will ever know as well as *you* is your mother or whoever raised you as a child. If that female lived alone in her realm, she was a queen. If you were not a royal child, who were you then and now? We are amazed at how many princes and princesses exist today. How can all of you reign? Some are actually regarded as royalty and placed on pedestals only to be besmirched at every crossing. Why do that? What is the point?

Your work is you, and if you do not work, you are not wanted. People who sit around all day are ignored. Look at idlers sitting on street corners. Do you believe others envy them? You need to rearrange your mind to consider the truth versus the envy of others who worked long and can take breaks from their work now. You, too, get breaks if you do work of worth. If you do not set out to make others envious, they will never begrudge you whatever.

What is it you want from us as your teachers? Do you want to sit and chat? Do you want a world-class essay contest? Do you expect a test? Why? What can induce you to work hard? The answer is: *Only your desire to do better.* No one else can motivate you, nor can you motivate others. Wise up now!

Where you learn is almost as important as when. If you are taught in a proper school, you believe you have nothing to learn elsewhere and shut down after school and seldom study again. If you skip school, you are forever trying to catch up to the imagined worth of those who did not. Be careful of skipping classes, it affects your mind more than your intellect.

Whatever you do, you do it as you are—at that moment. If you are precise—never miss a trick, or you can see through density of thought, your mind is constructed to do that. We cannot change your mind. You can change it, but no one else can.

How would you change your mind? You work at it. You study in order to understand why you are as you are and why an old way is not doing the best job for you now. You question how something can be used to change everything and make it better. That is how to change you—and it works!

The only thing missing from Today is time. You should know all about time since we lectured on it at great length in our last book, **Now is The Time.** It remains a part of your present world and a part of the concept of Tomorrow. That is why we will end this session within a short time. We do not want you to work on time until Tomorrow. (We jest, of course!)

The only time you can help others is if you know something they do not know, or you have more time to spend on the problem or have greater strength now. All other attributes are unnecessary when an intelligent person is stumped by a problem. The mind will produce new ideas and work out a way to do whatever is necessary with the limited resources at hand.

If your money is not abundant, you usually have a lot of time—or vice versa. God provides you always with the means to finish everything you start. Sometimes you do everything yourself, but sometimes if another knows how to do the work better than you, you help them learn by hiring or rewarding them well.

As you age you are not as easy to hold in hand—the teeth become sharp as well as the mind. If your mind is sharp and your teeth can rip food to shreds, money is less likely to bother you. If you are dull-witted and cannot chew, you get upset by everything and everybody from time-to-time. *(Not clear what is meant to 'hold in hand'? We are referring to the idea of keeping you in check.)*

Your body is not the only means by which you move. First you move in spirit, then mind, and finally the body moves when told to do so. You think the body needs to be toned and primed? You are who moves and does it—not the body itself. Why prime and preen when you need not do a thing to get moving? Vanity! Vanity is the cause of more social misery than greed—believe it or not.

In long lines of traffic you can let others go in front of you—unless they act superior. You can ignore everyone you meet—unless they snub you. You cannot exist if you are upset. Remember that! You must not let others expose you to hate or decisive actions that harm your mind or body in order to excel at a race of some kind. No one else will serve the sentence you bring upon yourself for vanity's sake.

You all say little about the life of a beautiful child, but some parents prance them around in exotic clothing or makeup, as if adults—even make a living off of them. That is not the way to train anyone. You will be held responsible for introducing vanity into the lives of children before they can tolerate such exposure.

You may or may not take a great deal of pleasure in dress and accessories, but if you cannot afford it—it is vanity. You can do whatever you like to your hair or nails, because they are dead tissue, but to mutilate the body's living tissue in order to decorate or enhance it in your society's image of beauty is intolerable.

Even pygmies are not exempt from envy. They favor the size of one person over another, but then again you believe they are savages. How can that be if they are like you? What you do to your hair and eyes is useless if it hurts, but many spend huge sums of money on a regular basis to look like someone else. Why? Vanity!

You say you need money, but what do you do with it? Do you spend it on frivolous things rather than necessities? If so, you are headed for: The poorest of dwellings and the meanest of diets. You must learn this now!

The World of Tomorrow cannot support the vanity of today! You will learn more about this as we go forward. We are jump starting the issue early so you will know how this work will help you prepare for tomorrow.

In the morning hours of each and every day people think that day will be long, but by afternoon they are making excuses for not getting their work done—and by evening there is no more time, if they are to be believed. Of course, such gross inadequacy does not exist. Time is! Time continues! All who labor continue until their work is done, be it today or tomorrow.

You need new work to help others decide why they are not going anywhere now. The greatest motivational tool we have found is one person doing something new. We originally ascribed it to envy and jealousy, but find at base it is curiosity. People are more curious than cats are reputed to be, yet do not recognize it in themselves. Why not set others on their heels by doing something totally unexpected?

You can surprise others!

When you wish to be noticed, do you stand up? We sense you do or you attempt to stand out in some other way. However, the best way to be admired is also easiest. Be yourself and learn to do your favorite activity to the best of your ability—it will make you a star!

Wherever you go, you learn, so go places and see many things. While living at home, learn household chores. Start out shopping and design a new life. It is all the same! Living occurs wherever you are. Learning occurs whenever you live. If you sit and relax, you may or may not think fast, but you are alive.

Work helps determine the direction of your life, but if your mind prefers a different direction, it can change it. The greatest deterrent on Earth to being who you truly are is sensing others disapproval of you. Why? You want to be liked—even though you dislike many others.

Why not like everyone and assume they like you? It certainly makes life easier! When you criticize others a lot, you feel and fear they do the same to you, but they do not. You are your worst critic! You do not need to be open and sincere, unless you want to open the door to your future. If you criticize everyone you meet, you soon learn they do not like to talk to you, either—and severely criticize you, too.

You learn that people can be mean. You learn life can be harsh—but you learn. Whatever you do, you learn. You learn by accepting life and by rejecting it. You learn by marrying—or not. You learn regardless of whether or not you attend school. Your life is a learning process—and you came to Earth to learn!

The price of learning is never so high you cannot afford it. You may not be able to rise to the grand heights your vanity prefers, but you grow. If your life is drab, you can always dream—and dreams come true sooner rather than later. We know that is true. Do you? Work on it and see if for yourself.

What you need now is a firm grip on reality as you believe it to be and a firm conviction that God is. Once you have those two concepts established in your mind, Spirit is free to delve deeply into the world of work and discover what you can do to improve this world and its work.

Wishes are not dreams!

What you do reflects the aim of your intellect as well as your dream. What you wish to do reflects only what you are not doing now. Wishes are not dreams nor work, thus they are of little use.

Work now to define Tomorrow and tomorrow arrives immediately! If you let go of the ideal setting for the rest of your life, you never move. You will sit endlessly where you are. You will vegetate and wish you had moved, but will not do it.

When you work hard at your life, you may see things change. You may see what you originally wanted is no longer good enough for you. You may decide you need more of whatever now. Why? Vanity! Your original dream was based on reality, but your wishes extended it into the future where you saw others with more of whatever and decided what you originally wanted was pale by comparison.

Finish one dream—then work on another. Do not adjust the dream until you finish your work on it, or you will regret it. Why not change a dream while it is being fulfilled? Your vanity or greed would be behind the change—not *you*. It will end a great idea with no greatness. Do not let others sway you from your dream and you will achieve greatness.

If projects usually end sooner than expected, what do you do? We sense many idle about looking for inspiration. We would like to caution you that this often leads to cancellation of projects already in queue. Let your mind's old work move forward first—only then release new ideas. You may find your old ideas are still fresh, active, and powerful. So why change them now?

If the work you do is dull and boring, you become dull—but probably not boring, unless you already are. From time-to-time you must refresh your mind with new ideas and new concepts or become outdated and passé, but do not rush to do so. You do not have to be up-to-the-minute on everything, but it helps to be familiar with a large number of areas that surround you now and are of interest to others. If you wish to maintain interesting friendships, you have to be interesting, too.

The last detail of this chapter to be covered is neither broad nor deep, but the most concise and shortest point we can make: *You have to know where you are now before you can decide where to go next.* Do not dwell on this thought too long, instead examine your life to see what you do well—and why and where it can be improved, then make necessary changes.

Once you know where you are—you are!

The only point left to make now relative to Tomorrow is that we will greet you there and ask if you did your work now. We see you as able to do it easily now—Do you?

Chapter Six

The only World of Tomorrow you can find now is the one inside your mind. It will not occur while you are on Earth because Tomorrow is a concept that cannot be achieved—only perceived. You believe in time, but time does not permit the aspect of *being* in advance of oneself in space, so you have to recognize that Tomorrow does not exist in your World of Today.

Why not write about Tomorrow and find yourself there? It can happen, but probably not. Why? There are so many variances and difficulties to comprehend that one cannot justify printing up a program for the event.

If any organization were to make plans for six months from today, would all members scheduled to be there attend? Would you want to print a program for the event now? No, you are aware of how much can happen to change things over a six-month period; yet many think nothing of asking others for a prediction about their lives months in advance. Why do you do that?

The only predictions that can stand up to reality are those involving a very brief span of time involving one—maybe two people, and only if they are alike and pulling in the same direction; otherwise, no chance of a prediction coming true for their mutual future.

If you cannot decide for yourself what you want—how can someone else decide your future for you? We encourage you to decide what you want, then design a plan that enables you to pursue your dream. What you do and how you do it are different ways of approaching the same goal, but differ in effort. You can be on one side of the fence one time and on the other side shortly thereafter if you wish to know all facets of life; but to make no decision and waffle back and forth constantly in order to see which side is better than the other is not wise. Select one side and go for it!

Your life is not written in ink, so it can be erased and written over if a better episode is found later. However, you cannot remove a life or erase it completely. If you attempt to totally encapsulate yourself in one episode of this life and not pay attention to any other part of your existence, you will end up imprisoned by it. The prison would be totally within your mind.

The moment you 'die', you have to be out of here and cross over to the other side. If you imprison yourself in this life, you will be unable to leave. Why bring this up now? Because you do not know what makes up your life now, yet you constantly ask about the future.

Perhaps if you knew what makes up a life you would not ask such questions? We will attempt now to describe the next life of any human being, so you do not have to die in order to experience death and know what we say is true. The pressure to believe in our work is great, because you know it is true...

You just know!

Once you cross over to the other side, you move forward into the tunnel of integrity and gain access to the holy light of God. If you are admitted, you cannot return to this life. If you are told to return, you will not remember it later. Some try to describe the fleeting visions and are accurate to a point, but most merely repeat what others say.

What happens next is not terrible, but most cannot speak of it later. You are asked to enter the next plane. If you can, you are asked to detail why you should be allowed to advance further now. If you cannot answer, your personal Spiritual Guide will help you respond— the Guide who helped you all the way through this life on Earth. Other Spiritual Guides who surrounded you during this life will also be on hand, but only one Guide is held responsible for the work you did or did not do while on Earth to spiritually advance your life.

While on Earth your life is not without a lot of murky water and dim lighting surrounding it, but once *'over there'*, all is exposed to the brightest of white light. You cannot hide anything. You are totally exposed, as well as everything you ever did here. Your insides are outside.

Your life here is held up and compared to the lives of those who also were here. If your life is far less developed or devoted to God's principles than the rest, you may not be able to return to Earth. Instead, you may be asked to step back into a less developed plane in order to work out where you stand in the universe now.

Work of The Holy Spirit is not the same as spiritual work. You do not get points for working in spirit, but you get lots of points for working to promote The Holy Spirit. Why? You must see how difficult it is to talk about God on Earth today to know it is not a time when spiritual matters are communicated well here, so if you tried to express your belief in God to others, you get a greater number of *points* for going against the pull of the world while here.

Many claim to be spiritual, but are not. Many say they are religious, but are not. Bear in mind you cannot remain spiritual or religious yet say nothing about God and your devotion to The Holy Spirit while here. You cannot! The time to begin speaking of God is when you have something to say. You are not the only one to speak of God, but be the only one who speaks to God for you! Remember, you must readjust *your* attitude—not attempt to adjust others.

Work is not *for* self, but on self. When you do your work, you cannot decipher which is You (the Higher Self) and which is *you*. Why is that? Because you are not separate beings—you are one!

In the process of dividing your mind into sections to accommodate all the data constantly being processed while here, you are placed in a terrible predicament. You need to recognize *you* and recognize that you are not *you* while on Earth. You are not on Earth to be *you* precisely, because you have to be you while here. You cannot run away from the *real you* or the *only you*, but you are expected to enjoy being this human version of You while on Earth. How can you do this?

Live in the NOW!

Whatever you do now is not as fast as living in the past or as slow as living in the future, yet it is. If you go back in time, you erase NOW. If you rush forward, NOW is erased. Thus, if you do not move out of Today, you remain here and live NOW!

What is it you seek? A life of ease and leisure, a time of repose, a lot of money? Whatever it is, you cannot take it forward with you. It exists only NOW! If you try to remove it, you will erase this time.

Ancient Egyptians were enamored with the concept of death. Issues they raised are still being debated. They never thought death happened to them—but it did. You do not believe in death, either, or at least make no preparations for it, yet you refuse to believe you live eternally. Much of the miscommunication over death has occurred since the times when the Egyptians ruled, but is now being erased. How? People continue to go back to the past to uncover its facts. Once they do that, the past is obliterated forever. You cannot go back!

Once you can see what was hidden, can you tell if anyone is there now? No, you cannot. You do not see anyone then, yet they exist.

You are not as delicate as you appear to be, but you are not as strong, either. Why? You cannot see entirely through you due to the density of material that makes up your body, yet your body is made up of chemicals that in themselves are not dense. How does science explain this? It does not. It expects children to accept that the body exists, materialism exists, and density occurs.

We want you to doubt science. We want you to become as skeptical of science as you have been of God. Once you are less gullible, look at theories you accepted too easily. What made you believe them? Why?

You were told to accept it by teachers you respected. We are teachers and we are here to unravel all the tall tales of this universe, but you need time to get to your teachers and correct their work. How do you do that? We cannot say.

What if your work has a major flaw, would you expect it to be corrected or would you fluff it off as being minor and unnecessary to correct it now? We cannot correct such major flaws as exist in your science now, because you all believe in Science! You do not necessarily believe it is all true, but you believe in Science—and that it is worthy of your total trust. Why? You do not wish to be bothered with dismantling the entire system now.

For several hundred years you all decided to believe in Newton and his theory of gravity. Why? It sounded reasonable—if a bit flawed. Now that you know so much more, why not change it? It would take time to do it. You do not wish to be bothered now. You have enough work to do already! All your excuses sound the same regardless of when or where you apply them.

If you think of God, and place Science before God, how do you justify the creation of the first placenta? Do you believe it just happened? Do you believe in total cosmic accident? That is unbelievable! You cannot believe there are no coincidences or that everything is an accident. It is so absurd an idea that it cannot possibly be enjoyed by humans today.

What if you were to go to bed and wake up in the morning and discover your world no longer exists, would you go back to bed? Not likely, but you might decide to pretend it is still here. Why? It would make more sense to you to continue a belief system that existed all your life than try to reconstruct a new one. As the New World nears, most people are living like that now.

We are not of the New World or New Age of Man

We are of another galaxy or universe and have never seen such a state of affairs as you have here, but we can readily understand it, because it is simple. You make it seem complicated, but it is simple!

Why not work hard every day? Sit out of sight and daily practice a bit of your work on self, then reenter the realm of your world renewed and restored. It would serve to keep you abreast of all that is and all that will be. We want you to prosper, but you must advance while here. If attaining prosperity is not conducive to spiritual growth, then you should reconsider the entire concept of *prosperity*.

What if you decide to visit the center of the universe and find nothing there? Would you want to return and tell everyone? Would you consider it shameful to tell everyone what only you know? Would you decide to sell the information? Which type of personality are you now?

We cannot deal with the type of people who are content to know knowledge exists, but try to suppress it from the masses. We are not happy to say much material has been channeled, yet not circulated or accepted by this world. We, too, are unsure if it is suitable for the masses, but hope it may serve some useful purpose now.

It is up to you, the reader, to decide if this material is to be decimated to avoid reeducation or served to the masses in heaps. What do you think about it now? We are here to serve the masses, but it takes several types of people to do it here and now: one to teach, one to preach, one to take it on the road to promote it, and one to tidy up all the loose ends. You could be useful in any one of these areas, but it is your decision to make—not ours.

What happens now will affect the future of your world. You cannot expect the world to remain the same, unless it rejects all we are here to teach. If it does that, we can predict several things:

1. The work of man will not prosper or develop beyond this point nor produce much of any value. If there is no concept of God, work is pointless and nothing spiritual remains in most societies on Earth.
2. The work of the world will not prosper!
3. Work of the elite will return to God's path, while all others begin seeking revenge. The elite will not be allowed to own everything. The world's first families will be eliminated and anarchy will be commonplace.
4. The work of a few will remain intact until a new civilization can be built. It may take several thousand years, but it will be done with only a few shreds and shards of this age remaining in place.

What you do on Earth is not your business! It is the business of us all. We are here because you do not plan to be here long, thus do not care what happens to this planet. Wrong! You will be here! You will be expected to clean up whatever you did wrong while here. You will be reduced to eating slime if that is all that remains to be eaten. You will be unable to end your lifetime here as easily as you can now, but you will have learned the consequences of a life misspent.

In the annals of your history are many times when people were spoiled by the facts of life. They grew to believe they could create life. You are now following that same line of thinking. Do you really believe you are the first to go down that path? Not likely, but egoists among you are sure you are pioneers.

Work on the day of this life when you were born. Do you remember it? No, you cannot. You were not born on a time-span of several days, but at a separate moment in time. You were preordained in that realm to be one separate being and have one special life, yet now you believe you can produce people on the average of one or two a day—and let *them* decide why they are here. *That is playing God!*

What about you? Do you play God? Do you insist on your way every day? Do you believe you deserve all you have, but others do not? Do you think others are unfairly or grossly overpaid? Do you think you are not receptive of the old ways, because you are brilliant? If you believe any of the above, no wise person could believe you!

Work is not the haven of the poor, but it is heaven to the wealthy. You cannot enjoy work or play unless you work at it. Can you enjoy leisure if you do not work? You need to plan to incorporate both concepts into one life. To seek only one or the other is a desperate attempt to ruin *you*.

We will not condone the ruination of anyone, but we see you often do. You place bars and houses of ill repute in the sight of innocents. You smoke opium or whatever and expect the population to support its consequences of laziness and crime. You do not expect others to pick up after themselves when they litter busy paths, instead pick it up for them.

We see you do not attempt to teach others the proper way to live, yet incarcerate any who go too far. Why? You love power! You feel none when you teach—only when you preach or destroy lives.

The goal of life here is to not idle!

You cannot break the fast of each night and move forward into the world without eating. If you work hard, fasting diminishes your strength; but if you eat more than you need, you will not work hard. You must learn to tolerate each other and eat what others eat so fewer crops are needed. Would you exist if you ate nothing? Yes, but not in bodily form.

Be ready to eat when you awaken and make sure it is enough, but not too much. Eat out of hand only what has been washed, and never eat during the rush of work. These are basics, but how many people abide by them now? Work and health are difficult to discuss today, because of your societies' differences. You do not offer equal opportunities to all of your people—or even the same food.

You need to streamline your communications and offer only one language the entire planet can understand and use easily. You cannot harm the rich, because they always discover what it takes to gain wealth, but the poor will be excluded if they cannot communicate easily. At the rate you are moving now, you will never learn to act as one people!

The Earth cannot sustain decades of fires ravaging the world's forests, yet you do not force anyone to stop setting such fires. All your lives are intertwined now and developing into a mesh, but you act as though you do not want it to happen. This is not wise. You must make plans to unite now!

The World of Tomorrow is not the only one we see, but what we see is invisible to you. You have to create it for yourselves. You are expected to know why you do what you do to Earth. You will be held accountable for it.

You will be sustained only as long as Earth can be maintained— not a day longer. You will not know the last day of Earth! Admit guilt for your part, then try to correct what you can and add to your spot of beauty now. This is the best any of you can do at this late date.

A day's work is not what keeps food on your plate, but if you do not work, food is not there. You cannot expect anyone else to feed you. God provides all you need, if you do your share, but others here are not expected to take care of you. You will benefit only if you pay your share. If you do not, you lose—maybe your life.

Why not admit you love life and then live like it? Why not begin a new life? Why not go forward into your spiritual path and grow in God? You are the only one to know why you would not. We can only guess if you choose otherwise and would not care to tell others why. You need to choose your destiny and let all others do their work, too. That is the way to live!

We have only one other point to make here and now. We want you to understand why someone would want to be here on Earth when the end of the planet comes to be. That person may have chosen to come here to help others leave. That person may be altruistic or Spirit incarnate, you cannot know now.

Be of good cheer! You have only one life to live and you can do it. Do not sit back and let others tell you they are not concerned about what happens in their lives. They definitely are concerned. We know!

What you do now determines your life—only. What we do now is of no concern to you, but we promise to continue to help you solve the riddles of Earth that hinder your progress as long as we can do so.

Chapter **Seven**

Whatever you do, do it well! If you do it only once, do it the best you can. If you cannot do it well, then do the best you can and let it go. If you could do better by doing it again, do it again—otherwise, let it go. Do not continue to try to correct what you cannot complete, and do not try to do anything that looks easy simply to feel happier than if you had tried something more difficult or complicated. This is the first stage of laziness—and it leads to a life of glittering defeat.

Be you!

Do your work and life is easy. Be someone you cannot be or will not sacrifice to become and you end up unhappy. Try to live inside *you* and see if life is not a lot easier now. If you do it right, you will find life is easier. If you suffer from growth, do not stop growing. Life is meant to be enjoyed as long as you continue to grow. The day you decide to end growth, you begin to die and life becomes less and less enjoyable.

Work and self-defeat seldom go together. Talk and much complaining ends in defeat more often than not, but to talk up something is likely to lead to its success. Salesmanship is needed to help business grow, and it helps you, too, but do not sell *you*. *You* are not for sale! Your goods, what you grow, and what you can do for others are for sale—not you!

When you decide to end your career, you quit or taper off your effort—both result in a genuine lack of interest in the business aspects of a career. You cannot be interested in something that has no bearing on your future.

When all of you decided to strip Earth of all its useable materials and elements, you let everything go, because you had no further use for the planet. Why be interested in Earth now? We cannot escape the consequences of our acts—nor can you!

Whatever you do, do not insist upon doing your work first and making everyone else wait until you are done. You have to share, because the last days are here. Without any further ado, let us share with you our view of Earth from here.

We can see Earth is a shell of materials long depleted—gold, silver, and other plentiful but beautiful precious metals once comprised the inner workings of the planet's electrical system. You robbed the communications core of its depth and cannot establish such communications now with other planets without going outside of your orbit. This was not necessary in previous worlds.

You produced a large number of clouds in the sky that elevated the temperature of the planet and caused severe damage to oxygen and other elements necessary for life on Earth. Why? Ego! Ego has destroyed more than all the other enemies of man put together. Thus ego (you, your mindful self) is its own worst enemy.

You are your own worst enemy!

Would you allow any enemy to enter into the workplace and tell everyone you are not any good at what you do now? No, you would discredit such a person immediately in an attempt to prove you are a competent person. But you do not stir when faced with the results of your incompetence in caring for this world you live in now and the planet where you reside.

Work is not the panacea for all that ails you, but it is the only approved remedy readily available. You need to do your work and stop forcing others to do what you can do yourself. You need to stop and look at all the things you have to do, then do them—one-by-one. No need to stop and look at the top of the wall or over the fence at others around you to see if they are working, too. You are who works for *you*—no one else.

If you cannot see, do you know what is going on around you? Yes, you can sense much that goes on around you—and are usually right. Why? The mind works even if you do not. If your body is hunched and bent, can you still work? Yes, the body can function until there is no energy left to convert into work. It knows not what else to do. If your spirit is broken and you refuse to refresh yourself, can you work? No!

Why expect the world's work to be easy?

You chose to come to Earth—or return to it in order to learn things you felt you needed to know before evolving beyond this plane. If you think you are hard on yourself now, you should hear others. You need to help and do what is obvious to others, but do not share all you have or do others' work for them. They have to do their work, too.

Mothers, in particular, are credited with doing too much of their children's work for them. This is often true, but seldom in the early years of motherhood. Why? A woman is seldom mature enough to work hard at being unselfish when young, even though she chose motherhood this life. To be unselfish is the hardest lesson to learn and it requires a large family to learn it well—and some will not learn it even then.

When you elect to do a lot for others, you may not do it for the best of reasons, but at least you are doing something with your life. When you do nothing for others, you will find no help when you need it. This is the method of measure: *You do enough for others to enable them to help others.* More than that and you produce an idler. Do less than that, you produce a needy person with esteem issues all his or her life. You have to help, but it is not help if you do it all.

Would you enter a contest and work very hard, then give the prize to someone else? No! You might win a contest and give the prize away, but you never give up what you work hard to attain.

What God gives is often wasted by those who receive it. Why? Ego! You have no right to give away what is given to you by God. It is your gift and must be appreciated and used by *you*—not given away. If you trade what you have, do you receive fair measure for it? Not often, so do not trade a gift from God for work of man. It is not the wise way to live today.

Workers are often placed in the middle of a dilemma. Who do you follow: the union of fellow craftsmen or the management that pays your bills? Think on this, too: When you owe someone money, do you plan to pay it back immediately or do you expect to pay it back in installments over a long period of time? If you are remiss in repayment, who do you think is hurt most? You are! You will be docked for such misconduct. You cannot harm another soul. It is held against *you*. You also find others do not pay you on time, too. The *'karmic law'* (as you say) is not that you get back exactly as you did, but are paid back in the same manner.

Whatever you do well, Do not share the news with all!

There are a few people who will share in your good times, more who will help in bad times, but few want to know of your success. Your mind is jealous of anyone who is better than you, but your spirit can overrule it. Your mind is a bit overwrought with what others have? Tell yourself to do better. If you cannot get this through to your mind, sit and meditate until you grasp the truth—then choose another path.

When you understand that all of life is a choice, and you are not required to do everything, you do one thing best. However, if you insist on doing everything, you end up being mediocre in all things.

Nothing big comes to those who sit and wait. Whatever you want to do—do it! You can sit and stare at the wall for days and see nothing. Instead go outside for a moment and enter into life. You have to change scenery or go stale, but you do not change other elements of life until you are completely done with them.

Some plan to make The World of Tomorrow one where no one is mated to another for life. Why? They are jaded and wish to sexually grasp others while maintaining their own freedom. Why? Ego rules them! You cannot maintain a friendship with another person forever without sex? Wrong! If you wish to live happily ever after, it is better to not have sex than have it with a member of the opposite sex. Sex is a means of communication not understood by man, and not much more advanced in animals.

You are surprised that sex is more advanced in the animal kingdom than in your realm? Why? You are not the superior being of the animal world—merely put in charge to see how well you manage all. So far you all get failing grades.

Some overproduce pets and kill them upon birth, some hurt animals for profit, some kill for fun and sport, some eat not what they kill supposedly for that purpose, some urge animals to kill other animals, some are so evil as to enter into sexual intercourse with animals, and some are not as fit to rule as the animal they are paired with for a time to see how they can survive as a team. You decide if any of this describes you and determine how much credit you will get when you cross over to the next plane and must answer for it.

No one is new to you! You may believe someone is a stranger, but it is not true. All of you are predestined by the cloning of the genes. If you had not been related to all on Earth, you could not be here now. All humans carry the same genes. No other beings are alike in the way humans are alike. Because of this, you have no one but 'you' all around you now!

This is the way of the world:

1. You have all you need, but want more.
2. You need nothing, but want what others say is better than what you have.
3. You do not want anything others would not steal.
4. You would steal if something meant a lot to you.
5. You think only things are stolen.
6. You know you have more things than you need, but continually ask for more.

Why is the world so preoccupied with *things* today? This is your decision—not ours. You decide and answer for yourself.

When you look at yourself, do you see *you* or the human you? The human likeness of *you* is what you actually see. If you design a new life, you grow to resemble it. If you design a lonely, old existence for yourself, you look like it. If you are mean and hateful, your face will betray you. If you work and push hard to get all you want, your body will resemble a battering ram. If you slide through life, dancing around the bad spots, your body will look like the body of a ballet dancer. First, decide what you want, and then grow into it.

What you need is not a new face or a new body. You need a new attitude. Today's attitudes are unsuitable for the next plane. You must learn to cope with malfeasance, yet not do evil. You must learn to cope with lazy people without becoming overbearing. You must learn to cope with those who vary from your way of thinking in every way without becoming a floor mat. You must learn to understand why you choose to do the things you do. Once you learn it all, you are *you*.

What you do now is not as important as it will be in the future. If you ignore this, you will have to learn it over again and again until you know it. Where you are now is not as important as it will be in the future, because it will determine how far you can go. If you slack off now, tomorrow will not be as advanced as it could have been. If you are severely handicapped, you cannot win races.

Why not work for yourself?

Why not become your own boss? You may not have the necessary coping skills, but you can learn them. Why not try? We are supportive of all who strike out and do their work now and hire others to assist them, because they are helping those who need a head-start while solving firsthand many of their lives' most complex puzzles.

The work of this day is not as well defined as it was in the past. That is not a problem, unless you have no idea who you are. Otherwise, you can devise things as you go along. It takes longer to get ahead this way—and there is a lot more waste, but you can still make progress.

What the world needs now is not love, but the use of the mind to employ its people—in order to deplete all the evil intentions now building up, and putting such energy to work building a better infrastructure to replace all that has been stolen from the Earth's crust. You cannot use what no longer exists, but you can make restitution and reap the rewards of the less original yet necessary elements still found on Earth. You must decide if Earth is going to be saved or junked. Remember, junking a planet is not a very serious matter to God, but to man it means the end of this world.

Although you seem to lack enthusiasm for living there, we welcome you to the work of reemploying your people in rekindling enthusiasm for the world you all built together. Why? You try to ignore the fact you are in charge of your life here and now, and steadfastly refuse to accept that responsibility. Why? Tell us!

If you make no mistakes, are you better than everyone else? Maybe—then maybe not. If you do not work, you make no mistakes, but if you do much work and make a few mistakes, you end up further ahead than those who never work and thus never make mistakes.

It is easy to use work as an illustration, but life is not as easy to explain. You must remember when you last thought an original idea and acted upon it. Why not do that every day? You could, but you do not like to spend much time in meditation. Why? You prefer to think—and think you know it all!

You are not true believers in God. You think, not believe, God is a good, benevolent being who decides things for you, but you do not believe you have to follow such guidance. Therefore, you do not believe! It is a very simple thing to see from this distance, but you prefer to be less forthright.

You prefer to live in shades of gray rather than white light. White light is not God. It is the power of God to transform all into the positive beings they are intended to be. *You* cannot transform anyone else, but you can include them in your circle of light. You may decide to live in your circle alone, but it is far better to enlarge it and enjoy the love of another—or three or four others.

Wonders are all around you!

Do you feel them now? Do you see them? Are you aware of the feeling of being surrounded by energy? No? Then you are not on *your* path!

To seek a path and not find it easily is hard on *you*, but wandering through your entire life on Earth unaware there is an easier path is stupid. You knew of the path to your destination before you entered this atmosphere. You can find it again at any time, so why stumble in the dark now? You do not want to take orders! You want to be childlike instead, letting others protect and provide for you.

You do not like to make decisions, thus avoid them because you want to be in on the last days of Earth. We cannot guarantee anyone will survive the last days of Earth. We have no way of knowing when or how Earth could end, but you all are trying to make it go off its orbital path and destroy itself by colliding with another major asteroid. What is so bad about Earth that makes you all so dim about what you should do to solve these problems now?

Work is the way to unite all people, but you all refuse to work together now. You war forever and ever, and no work that could unite everyone interests you all now. Work and war are the two primary ways humans have available to coexist, but war enslaves captives and enlarges the egos of winners so much that it destroys you all—so war is not the way to go! Peace, along with work, is the best way to enact a lifelong siege of all that is evil. However, most are unaccustomed to the ways of peace and fear they will end up being captured and forced to work if they do not prepare for war instead.

You sentence criminals to hard labor. Why? You believe it is the worst of all possible fates—outside of death. Your two penalties happen to be the best means of entering the next plane. What do you think of that?

The World of Tomorrow

You might rehabilitate criminals, but it is not in your plans to do so now. Instead you prefer to end their lives. You wish to end all their prospects. You do not want them to come out of prison and prosper. Why? You envy them their lack of work, while they envy you your ability to work.

The time to end another session is here, but we have not ended our discourse on the future of *you* and your kind here, so we will end for now on this note: *If you have nothing to do, you will not be able to finish this book.*

You may have to stop reading now due to work, but it will haunt you otherwise and force you to return and read all that is here. Why not agree to work and read this book now? You can do both!

Chapter **Eight**

The only person not upset by The World of Today is one dying or not living in the present. If you ignore all that is NOW, you may not be here tomorrow. You must live each day as though it was today—not tomorrow! If you wait, you may not be able to enjoy anything.

To wait until tomorrow to start living is not sane. You do not know if tomorrow will arrive or not. You can only be sure of NOW—which is not as apparent, but the only time you have to live.

Whatever you do for yourself is done. Whatever you do to others may not be. If you are in their debt for anything, you will have to repay it one day or be unable to advance. If you refuse to repay debts while here on Earth, you will know poverty in the future. If you do not care about the future, you will not pay bills in the present. If you do want the future free of debt—karmic or otherwise—pay as you go.

One of the worst kinds of debt you can accumulate is one of money owed to lenders. You cannot expect lenders to care if you can afford to repay it or not. It is your privilege and honor to repay whatever you borrow. To expect a lender to extend time or money so you can repay a debt is foolish and leads to further hardship. Please review your debts and repay all of them before you borrow again. You cannot end life in debt and expect to be advanced. It is a definite sign of a bankrupt life.

What if you advanced money and no one repays you? You have been foolish beyond belief, but you are not harmed. You gave what you obviously did not need or you gave to impress others, so you will not be upset because another did not repay you. You will not be held responsible for lending money to help others, unless it was to deepen their debt or lead them off their individual life paths.

When you borrow from another, you expect to die before you have to pay it all back, but you usually live. The lender expects you will live long enough to pay it all back. Who would you rather think like now? We honor those who trust people enough to give them money for what is needed in life; but if it is not needed, they can hurt their own chances of advancement.

It is said in your world: *"Be neither a borrower nor a lender."* Wise words often quoted, but more often disregarded by common men and women—yet uttered frequently by the wisest and richest of all societies. Why? Either way it leads to greed.

When you are in debt, you spend more than you would if you were not. Why? You become desperate and tired of being in debt and fail to recognize the power it has over you. You begin to shirk responsibilities and expect others to help you. You live from one stipend to another and ask for help in-between times. Why? You are not living for *you*. You are trying to be someone else, or you do not want to be free.

Freedom comes to those who owe nothing!

If your life is entangled in a web of money and personal relationship problems, you cannot free your mind. You try to extract every bit of work from it you can, but cannot relax and enjoy the life you have. For this reason, we offer you a simple way to immediately relax: Be you!

If you are sick and tired of being someone else, you are you. You cannot be you and enjoy acting like someone else even for a short time. You cannot act or be another personality without it extending into your *'auric field'* and leaving false or negative impressions. Why would you risk becoming a role you are acting rather than being you? You believe this life is not worth living.

When your life on Earth is over, you will never be aware of the times you were not here and had to hold up others who were. You will not be aware you, too, often visited others here on Earth to support them in their need. It is too often the case now that humans demand attention from those on other planes, seeking help with their earthly jobs. We ask you to stop interfering with others elsewhere who have much work to do, too.

What you ask for and what you get are the same, but too often you change your mind or forget what you originally asked for or prayed about to be grateful when you receive it. You cannot become proficient and efficient if you do not do your work. You may be helping another advance, but so what? Why do you worry about others getting on in the world when you are not? Ego! Your ego would like to believe you are superior to others—and you are not. Obviously, others think the same about you, but you seldom see it that way. Why?

What you need to do this life is ask for help when you need it—and never ask for help if you do not. It is a simple proposition to ask, but not easy to receive. You are expected to give back what you do not need and may end up in debt if you give too much. Whichever route you take, you are not even. If you seldom ask for anything, you will have whatever you need and can get what you need easily—and quickly. Do not abuse it and you will always have plenty to use. You may or may not realize what we mean now, but as time goes forward you will.

The future is based on Today—and Today too many are wasting Earth's natural resources and not paying enough attention to it. Why would God be so sure of *you* being of such worth as to let you destroy Earth? You (the Higher Self) are of God, thus cannot be destroyed here. Earth is a planet created by God for your use, and if you abuse it, you lose it. What is abused and neglected might be revived, but seldom is.

We think the older you grow the more likely you are to begin to conserve energy. Nature absorbs the fact that you are less and less demanding of the environment as you age. However, some never learn and waste much up to the day of their last breath on Earth.

Why not let up and end your life early? We see some doing that now who will end up returning to Earth to finish all they came to do now. You, too, have no idea what you have to do here until you are no longer on Earth, so do not act as if you do know.

When you are told one or two things about why you came to Earth or what it is you came to do, do you automatically feel pride in knowing it? Why? You are not done here! You cannot say you have done it all. You cannot take pride in what is not done. You have to work at this life every day until you leave Earth, in order to finish, and you do not know if you did it all until it is too late for you to do more work.

Work is why you are here!

You may believe you enjoy total freedom from labor or stress now, but you do not. No one can sit and do nothing! To sit still and do nothing is too hard on your physical and mental well-being. Only the spirit of man is happy to sit and do nothing but meditate for days.

You must learn to develop silence within, yet most cannot until late in life—even then most struggle to maintain it for hours at a time. Meditation then becomes their work. If young, your work may or may not be physical in nature, but it is still difficult to meditate.

When an anxious person works in the world of business, all notice how easily distracted that one is. You may or may not believe you are easily distracted now, and if you cannot meditate easily, acknowledge it is true of you. Why be offended by the suggestion that you cannot meditate? You constantly offer this excuse as a child might whenever you do not want to work spiritually, even though you know it is unworthy of *you* to make such excuses, because you can meditate if you try.

Where you fit into the scheme of things is not of equal importance to each person, but it is of great importance to the powers controlling the effects of work and this world. Do not stare down anyone and refuse to do whatever you came to do. Do your work daily or expect to not survive long in this world.

The only world you live in is here and now, but you hunger and thirst for the future like a camel preparing for a long journey. You cannot know how long the trip will take you, but are busy preparing for it now. This is wisdom!

What you need to do to be ready for the future is here and now and requires adjustment daily. If you do nothing for several months, can you easily pick up the pieces again? Not if your work needs daily attention. If it requires only a little bit of attention now and then, maybe so. Only God knows.

What you do spiritually is your work, and you are not too busy to do it! You cannot exist without doing your work. To ignore the body or soul leads to dementia of the mind. To ignore the mind's work leads to deterioration of the soul—sometimes even the body.

The soul can take a lot more abuse than either the body or mind, because it is the core of your being. At the center of any universe is a core of cells which are unlike the rest of that being. This core is seen as the nucleus of the egg or center of creation. Remember, your Earthly body is not the center of your universe—your soul is. You will never spot it here, either.

You often tire easily when you work spiritually. If you do no such work, you will become unable to do anything quickly. It requires practice to maintain what you have here, if you wish to keep it. If you do not maintain your spiritual life while here, you lose it!

To decide to end a life is never easy, but it is necessary. You will never be told to end your life here because another one has arrived. You will never be told to go on and end your life, because you made a mess of this one. You will never be told to end your life ever!

It is the concerted effort of all areas of your total being that determines when this phase of existence no longer serves your needs and can be safely ended. If you decide to end it now, you will short circuit your entire being and require a major attack of the universal glutamine plasma to heal before it becomes fact. You are not to cause such a rupture—ever!

When an ego decides to seek a premature ending to a life problem, it is decided mentally and requires the body to cooperate, but Spirit often surfaces and denigrates that impulse. Why would you want to kill your body? Because you neither appreciate it nor believe it is of God.

You are of God—unless you have achieved the distinction of alienating God. Why would you do that? Only your mind knows for sure. If your body is overheated and confused by anger, you may alienate others on Earth, but be sure you say nothing about God. Such defamation can lead to eternal damnation of your soul. Yes, it can!

When a body of light is struck by lightning, what happens? You become so concentrated in the light that the body may disintegrate—or not. It all depends upon the concentration. If life is a bolt of lightning and you are physically weak, it may help you or it may not. If you are very strong by nature and have added much strength to your body, you do not need a lightning bolt to strike to ignite you now. You can disintegrate and rise above this vaporous atmosphere—even return again. This is not impossible, but highly unlikely today.

If your body is of light and very bright, you can be seen clearly from above by the 'heavenly host'. If angry and upset, you flash brilliant shades of red which alert all to the danger you pose to yourself as well as others on Earth. The angels often *fly* to your side to make sure you do nothing rash then, but you can still do something unwise. Angels can only step in and help if you ask God for help. No one can interfere in the life of another being—not even angels or archangels!

You have to realize you are responsible for all you do and all you say aloud. When thinking something, you may never be heard by anyone else, but then again maybe you are heard. It all depends upon how powerful you are at the time. If you think an evil thought, it may enter the airways and be heard or not. If you utter positive words of encouragement or pray for another's rescue or salvation, you will be heard even if you never say a word. Why? You glow as you pray!

Damage done to man is most often caused by the ego and seldom results in permanent lifelong injury, but it can happen. If you injure another so seriously they cannot function, you will be held accountable for it. You may escape detection while on Earth, but the entire universe knows you did it. No one gets away with murder!

You may believe others have nothing you want, then see some little thing that must be yours. What do you do? Do you pray? Do you ask aloud and seek another who may help you attain it? Do nothing about it? Steal it?

Obviously, you get into severe trouble whenever you steal, so do not do it, but what about getting it from another by guile? You are not to demand things from others. If another has to steal or resort to other anti-social behavior not worthy of you to get what you want, you can depend upon it that you will suffer for it, too. You cannot buy what has been stolen, hoping to keep it, and not be judged to be as guilty as the thief. If you permit another to do that for you, you will become the victim of fraud or abuse, too.

When you decide to end your life episode on Earth, you may also decide to recall every single thing you ever did here, which is unnecessary. You will have time to do whatever on the other side and do it much more efficiently then. If you can let your past go when it is time to cross over, do so and go forward undaunted. Do not tarry at the end!

What you do now prepares you for the next life. If you do nothing now, you can still go forward—provided you did no evil to anyone while here on Earth. Evil is not your source of God gone wrong, but the ego leading you into the sins of the flesh that constitute most human problems. Do what you can to rectify old sins, and do what you can to erase the effects of any evil you may have inflicted and maybe you can advance above anyway. To do nothing about evil you committed while here, you will immediately return to Earth to learn that lesson!

When people die of what you call old age, you may believe they have a long, easy death because they died late in life, but it may be they could not cleanse this life's slate and had to take much more time to do all they came here to do. Whatever reason a person has for lingering long on Earth is not to be discussed as fact. Only YOU knows when *you* are ready to go, and only YOU will say it is time to go!

If you add all the things you did while on Earth to the stack of what you did elsewhere, you have the entire output of your soul. If you take away a lot of energy from that pile now, you may bankrupt your eternal soul. It is not wise to spend what you do not have here and now, since it can result in a return to Earth to finish what you were trying to complete this life when you ran out of energy.

What if you died of old age without anything in this world to add to your soul's productivity? We doubt it can happen, but if it were possible, you would still advance. You would be in dangerous territory, but it could be you took nothing, either—so you end up even. It is the 'karmic debt' load that pushes you into needing to return to Earth for further work—not the lack of good work.

When you enter this work you enter the world. However, you do not end your work when you leave the world. You merely begin a new phase of spiritual growth. You enter a new and more difficult phase of development based on what you learned while on Earth, but not related in any way to it.

Why would anyone want to enter another plane now? You get to the point where you earned as much and learned as much as you can, and to stay here is detrimental to your entire being and could lead to deterioration. You need to grow to thrive and stay alive. Once you stagnate, you flounder and fall in vigor and health. You need to move and work to survive on Earth, as well as elsewhere.

This is the hardest plane to leave, because of the negativity here and around the planet, but it is not the most difficult of all your soul's assignments. In fact, it is so enjoyable here that some decide to stay long after they cease to learn or grow. Now they *must* leave to provide a place for those who have to return to Earth to live in health.

Earth cannot support this many people!

The reason Earth became overpopulated is obvious to some, but not to humans. The 'Age of Man' on Earth was seen as almost over, yet many souls had not experienced it and wished to be here, so they entered bodies as soon as they became available. You can believe birth statistics increased because of modern medicine, but it was the flow of souls demanding entrance that lies behind the increase of population all over the world. Man cannot stem the flow—only God can.

When you abort a fetus, you are not aborting a soul, unless the time of entrance of the soul has arrived—and that can happen at any time up until the actual birth. Most souls enter a fetus sometime near the third trimester in order to get a feeling for the connection with the mother and to live within her womb to determine if life will be suitable with this woman. If not viable, that soul ends the pregnancy. The woman who ends a pregnancy is in no mortal danger, if she ends it soon after it begins, but she could harm her soul if she waits. To demand such an abortion is to be aware of the consequences, but to neglect a child once born is far worse.

Adoption and the disposition of children to homes other than their natal parents' abodes is never wise, but sometimes necessary. We would never want you to do such a thing, but it can be done safely. If you fear death may result if the child remained in your care, you should make sure it has a safer home. If you give up a child for ego pleasures or work of the world, you will not be blessed with greatness in that child. Children require unique attention—and distractions can be harmful. If your child is cared for by others, you need to be aware you are still held responsible—always, with no exceptions.

What we need from you is a blessing for this world and all who reside within its realm, but before you can prepare such a blessing, you have to first feel blessed. A child often makes adults feel a great miracle occurred in their lives, thus they cannot respond in the proper way to control and discipline the child when necessary. We regret such neglect, but it is not nearly as serious as when adults hold no esteem for the child and tear its mind down daily for selfish reasons.

The child of today is Tomorrow's man or woman and requires a lot more education than ever before. Soon they will be able to do a lot more spiritually than you can do now. Why? The beings now arriving on Earth are more and more advanced! You may or may not be one of them, but you need to know they are here and arriving in greater numbers so they may complete their Earthly requirements, too. If you should be lucky enough to have such a being in your life, you will have no problems raising or correcting this child, but you will have to provide such a child with a high-level lifestyle or they will reject you.

Not one soul on Earth deserves less than the best of everything, but too often some think they deserve more than others. This is ego and not to be condoned. Remember to keep your ego in check—always!

When you enter the next plane, you will know more about what you did on Earth—and why, than you do while here, but you cannot correct anything then. It will be too late. Truly, you need to keep your daily diet and health on target and live a mentally-stimulating social and work life, but it is the spiritual elements of this life that later benefit you the most in your work on higher planes.

Use your time here wisely!

We are not done with this plane once you leave Earth, and you may be asked to help others still here. Remember, you had Spiritual Guides while here and refused to use their advice or follow their directions. Be prepared to feel the same rejection. Be prepared!

What you cannot see while on Earth now will be revealed, but you may find it is not what you expected to learn. It depends upon how in touch you are within your soul—so connect to your spiritual source as much as possible now so it is not a huge shock.

This session is overlong, and not as concentrated on this world as most, but reveals the direction taken throughout this book. Do not reveal anything to others who follow you, since they are not ready for it. However, you can urge readers to continue working when the going gets tough or when they tire of studying and doing homework alone.

This is homework—and you do it alone. No school on Earth teaches you how to live your life. It is entirely up to *you* to do. Be ready for more of the same from us—but rest now.

Chapter **Nine**

The only old ways to be remembered now are those that benefit tomorrow and Tomorrow. The world now uses so many different things in very unusual ways due to the past, but the future will be simpler. The world will learn to rely on truth—and wrong ways will be dropped. The only old ways to use are those that work now!

There are those who aspire to erect temples to the knowledge of today only to discover they are outmoded by next week's construction. Why? Greed forces them to advance before they have it all figured out. If you work toward the completion of a project—and finish it, nothing further can be changed. If you work only part-way through and publish it as being done, anyone can change it completely.

When you feel you know it all, you immediately discover you are wrong. If you believe you know little, you often realize you need lessons in only a few areas to make sense of the whole subject. Why? Life is a classroom and 'A' students are not smug or glum. They are searching for knowledge. They believe they do things of worth—and they work at it, while 'F' students are not into the game and usually drop out.

What if you sensed you had the means to be the best at what you do, but no one else cared? Would you continue to work and do whatever it takes to do it better? Probably not, but you could. Why would you stop? Ego! *The Spirit of All* wishes to work on what is best for the individual, but ego wishes to impress all regardless of what is best for the individual. It is *you* who decides who is in charge!

Where you are and what you do there is not the cause and effect of life, rather a reaction to your personal behavior. You do not have to work hard, but if you do, you go farther than those who do not. If you idle and meditate on the subject of God and Man as opposed to life within the fast elements of society, you will find one man develops socially and the other spiritually. Can you expect to develop evenly if you walk both paths? No, you will eventually give up one or the other, but the life you then pursue is better for the change. You will know more about this as you age, because as you age you decide to leave one personality for another and one stage of development for another, simply as a matter of course.

What if you felt you could never do all you came to Earth to accomplish? Would you give up? Probably, so you are not told. Work on what you have to do each day and the following day is full of accomplishment, too. One day builds upon the other, so you cannot ignore the work of one day and end up further ahead the next.

If you are a success, it is not important where you are and who you know. If you are not successful, you want to know who you can be in order to discover who you will be. That is why models are needed now! If you cannot model good behavior, then be all you can be and help others in different ways—but modeling good behavior is best.

When your life is over, and you left this plane, you will know all you came to learn, plus a few things you may wish you had not learned. Why? You do not need negativity in your work then to bring out the positive. You had to learn how to use negativity while here, because it can short-out energies. This plane is where you learn to combine the two poles over time and will learn to use positive light as a source of energy long and wide of this plane.

Your knowledge of positive and negative charges is of obvious use in this world and in the work you do here, but the use of negative energy is of little value elsewhere in the universe. You need to adapt— not adopt the negative ways of man to learn how to live here, but walk away from such things whenever you can in order not to be condensed.

You will be all you can be if you try!

To accept the status quo as being the status quo is *The Error* of most living on Earth now. You begin to accept it and believe it is true, but it is not! You can change the entire being of Man by being yourself. However, if you refuse to change, mankind remains the same to you as always and continues as is until you leave this world.

Wherever you go you will see others trying to get ahead of others in line—at work, in traffic, wherever, but they do not get far before those waiting are beside them. So why bother to rush and compete with others? It is an ego thing to compete—not of Spirit. You want to know you are good, but you need to realize others are good at what they aspire to do, too. If you are mature (wise), you will help others help themselves get ahead and never be envious of their success.

This work is not of this world, But prepares you for the next one!

You need not spoil others to get what you want. You may believe you must coddle others or manipulate them in some way to work, but you do not. Simply tell them what needs to be done and when. That is work and what all expect when they farm out their labor. You hurt all if you believe everyone wants what you desire.

If your life is different from when you started out, you made it that way. Your life is a picture of you—not someone else. If you like to say someone else chose your career for you, you are inaccurate. If you imply someone else told you about the career you are pursuing and you have no other career in mind, this is true. Always be honest with *you*! Others may or may not be honest, but if you are, you grasp life by the throat and will not get lost.

Your life is not a threat to *you*, but you often imagine others' lives are a threat to yours. Why? Ego! Your ego is a threat to *you* more than any other human being could ever be. You let it grow so huge you cannot imagine who or what it is and why you are as is—only then do you pray for guidance. Why not tell your ego who *you* really are and let your Spiritual Guides help you grow in the path of true belief in You and God? Life is so simple then!

What some desire now is a lifetime of adventure and intrigue. They have to have it at any cost, while others do not. You must decide which line of intrigue you can accept or be overrun by those who plot and scheme all the time. Rats of the Earth are not plotters or schemers, merely animals making their way, but humans acting like rats can be vicious. You should not let *'rats'* run your life. If you do, you will be trapped here, too.

Where do you go if you cannot advance to the next plane or return to Earth? That is not often thought about now, because it is of little use to most on Earth. You seldom do anything so bad that you would be expelled from God's sight, but it happens.

What to expect if you are expelled? You will not be told anything. You will have nothing to do. You will idle in space, and time will be locked in a position of idleness until all eternity is gone. This may appear as totally incomprehensible, but it is!

What you do now is what you will do in the future—good or bad. You may succeed if you try to change now, but maybe not; however, movement will advance you. Obviously, stillness is the opposite of movement.

Silence is not stillness. You need silence in order to deposit your life in its appointed space, but you do not *need* to move. Once you are still, you become nothing. You fade into the atmosphere. You are a vapor. If you move, you beget energy, and energy begets power, and power begets use of *The Energy* and *The Power*.

Never put your life on hold!

Do not sit still nor watch others work, unless you are learning how to do the same work. If you sit and do nothing, the body will severely atrophy and die away. Why? Its sole purpose is to move you about to do your work, and if you do not work, it is not needed.

Why sit and stare at others having a good time? It may help you learn to enjoy yourself, too, but not likely. You need time to adopt social behaviors needed to participate in the world—and such time is well spent if it enhances your well-being then. If it depresses or otherwise converts your energies into negative pursuits, obviously you harmed yourself. Let life teach you its work, then do all you came here to do. That is how to leave Earth and move forward!

Work of *The Holy Spirit* is not as dense as Earth work, but it takes more energy. You have to travel great distances within your spirituality—and it takes energy to travel. Before you can end a life on Earth, you need to end your dependence upon people you established here. This is the Earth's way of helping you learn independence. If you cling to someone who fails you or leaves you, you learn more than if you walked away from them first. If you must learn both lessons, the latter will be harder than the first. However, both are necessary to become independent of others!

If your life is not going the way you hoped, stop and look at it, then continue in a totally different direction. If your life is going well and all are happy with you as is, why change? Your ego may decide it needs more room to expand—having become too big for the cramped confinement of your home or family life. Be sure you are ready spiritually to soar, before you decide to drastically change or *you* will crash to Earth.

When you see others try new things, do you hope they succeed? If not, you are too attached to this world and thus fear others. If you hope they succeed—even help them achieve some of their goals, you do not fear their lack of dependence on you, because you are mature (wise). What if you have mixed emotions about such things? You are learning and growing—a wonderful combination!

In The World of Tomorrow you will be unable to complain about work since you do everything yourself. How can you stop such complaining now? Simply do not complain! If negative comments come to your mind more and more easily, try to rectify the mood, fear, or feeling causing it. Do not let it continue!

Sometimes you are unaware it is necessary to change. If you let things accumulate and begin to feel uncomfortable as complaints of body, mind, and spirit build, and you utter complaints about them—act! Be sure you act with full accord or you may end up behind wherever you were.

Complaining opens the airways to a new beginning. If a complaint is not worthwhile, you need to end it. If it is worthwhile, you need to change something.

Work is often the first area to reflect change of atmosphere here. If you do not like where you work, you may actually be reflecting on the air or lack of oxygen. If you cannot breathe properly, you hunt for another spot. It may appear to be disappointment in the job, but actually is a physical need to be elsewhere. Before leaving, work to clear the air at home, office, factory, or farm—to make sure it is not why you wish to leave.

More and more of Earth is polluted by oxygenic systems lacking sufficient oxygen, yet people are expected to breathe within them. Before you re-circulate air, be sure it is not foul or death can come quickly to all present. Some airplanes are safer than homes, but some are not. If the air is befouled, how can the crew work in it? You never know if it is the cause of death in an accident or not, since other areas could also be weak and thus are blamed instead.

People today do not believe a lack of oxygen is damaging their brains. What you eat and drink now affects your future. Within the body's power, energy is converted into action. If you eat nothing worthy of you, how can you grow better? Eat well today so tomorrow is built on a good body that can react quicker and better to all complaints of its own making. Let your body rot or vegetate in alcohol and fat and nothing good will come of it.

What you eat is of great importance, but what you see is also important. Be sure to look at great art as often as possible in order to refresh the retina and cornea of your eyes. The past etches itself on the interior of your eyes and cannot be erased. You need tears—lots of them—to erase pain, sorrow, or indecency. However, if you choose to cry a lot, hoping to forget the past, it may turn into a deep depression—which is never a popular way to live in Today's world.

Depression is not about today— It's all about yesterday!

Depression cannot help you move up or move forward—only cling to your past. If you wish to quickly move up and forward into the future, drop the past each and every day. If you do not, you will in time become overwhelmed with stimuli which depresses your activity level to such an extent you cannot move. Learn to finish each day's work and leave it behind, so you can more easily move forward.

Why would anyone want to stay locked in the past? Tomorrow scares them! If you could lock yourself in one room, which would you choose: Today, Tomorrow or Yesterday? Most choose the past, meanwhile the present becomes the past tomorrow. If you are chronically depressed, opt to be locked into the future.

The difference between depression and oppression is that one is done solely by you and the other by another. Actually, the choice is yours—neither has to be. It is you who empowers others or refuses to use the power you have. Be of good cheer and all is yours to direct!

Being filled with fear robs you of all you have here. No one here can take away your eternal being or your spiritual life, but some still try. You must take control of you or *you* will be swept away by the enthusiasm of others around you.

If you let others direct you in the work of this world, you might prefer to be directed in your spiritual work, too. Instead, why not sit and create a list of everything you need to do and prioritize it, then do them one-by-one? The lazy man will say: *"I don't have time to get organized."* The honest, hard-working person is organized and uses a mental list if not a material one.

This is how to succeed:

1. Put your home in order and keep it that way.
2. Put your life in order and keep it that way until it becomes cumbersome and requires major change.
3. Pull your weight and never expect others to do your work.
4. Put your heart on hold if your life is not flowing well.
5. Project your mind into the world if you need information.
6. Free your Spirit!

When you do all these things, you are a happy human being! You have no doubts, no fears, no health problems, and no lack of success. You will be *you* and enjoy all this life and be ready to move on at the end of this time on Earth. However, if you lack movement in any of these areas, at that point you are hung up and need to work it out, before you can move forward.

Why would you hinder your progress? You want out of your life here, because you do not understand *you*. You want out of the mess you created due to a series of miscommunications with You (your Higher Self), thus end your work here. Before you can end this life, you have to do all you came here to do or be returned to do it all—plus a lot more. Which life is obviously best for *you*?

You may say this world is not all one race now, but it is. There is only one group of animals on Earth known to be human, and you are one of them. You may differ in sex, size, or color, but you are all human. You will be human as long as you are on Earth, but you will not be human once you leave. Is this really that hard to believe or understand? Why ponder it so long? Because you are human!

Put your humanness to the test and die. Give up! Put your shoulder to the moon and try to move it. Whatever else you think you are, you are only human. You may think you are here for this life only, but you are not. You can develop further on Earth than elsewhere right now, but it is not the only place where you develop.

Your life will be out of this planet's orbital path long before your orbit ends. You, too, are a planet in a major galaxy. Earth is in itself a major organism that breathes and lives, even though you act as if you live here alone.

Welcome the sun...Live on Earth...But remember, you are only human.

Put your life under a microscope and what do you see? Sickness is not present, nor anything strange and undecipherable. You are made up of tissue and matter still unidentifiable to humans, but it is still you. You are no larger or smaller because of close scrutiny, so hold your life up to the telescope's lens and see if it grows. It does not, but if you meditate, you can see all of you—and *you* then grow!

This lesson on Today is one of great interest to many, because it answers some of the small concerns you have about life on Earth. However, you overlook the fact you are here for only a short time and then gone—and you have to do all this life's work before you leave. Be sure you do it all now, or you will be coming back again and again.

Meditation is a clearing house of fact and fiction. If you add it all up, no other work you do during any given day gives you as much of whatever you seek as meditation, but it needs to be done daily! So pull up a chair, sit on the floor, stand quietly on the bus—whatever, but meditate every day as often and as long as possible, if you want to insure you will get all your work done on time.

When you meditate twice a day for ten or fifteen minutes each time, you are merely resurfacing your mind—not elevating or changing it in any real way. If you meditate for an hour or more at a time, the mind feels enervated, but it is your spirit that soars to new heights.

You are always in charge, but the mind grows restless and tired if captured and forced to relax. Make sure your mind relaxes as often as your body requires rest and never have a mental breakdown. As you meditate, what you meditate on is of no consequence. Once the mind is free again, it will know exactly where to go for any information you seek and quickly handle such matters. When your mind overflows with distracting data and stimuli, you cannot think effectively.

In the future, if you wish to stimulate the mind and retrieve what you need to work effectively and efficiently, be sure to meditate longer than usual. When you meditate more than three times daily, or over an hour during any given day, you feel refreshed—and at odds with no one! You will be calm, cool, and centered! You will not be easily upset by anyone! Your work will flow and all will glow! You will not be the same as you were before you started to meditate that day.

You grow as you meditate!

Where the skull meets the neck is an area of pain for some. It is not that the skull is heavy or the neck is not strong, it is due to the way energy slows there in order to enter the spinal column. Please sit erect at all times and let your energy flow. If you meditate in any other position, you hinder the direct flow of energy to the brain and back again to the body. Be sure you know your body well enough to seek out those spots where energy is not flowing and correct them immediately.

What you do now is not important, as long as it grows toward the light of God. If you direct your life in any other direction, you will fail. You may reach a substantial height before the shallowness of your root system fails, but it will happen. For most, you cannot grow tall from shallow roots. It is a waste of time and energy to follow anything but the light in this life.

Work today on this material and you will know what to do tomorrow. Sit and stare at this book and you will not. Be alone and meditate for a short time now or run out into the world—never again able to recapture this moment in time. Each decision is yours! You are responsible for each of your days here on Earth. You can never say you had no time to meditate, because you do!

As we think about why we cannot begin another chapter if the last one was not completed, let us go to the next chapter.

Chapter Ten

The only work done on Tomorrow is the work of Today! The only time you should be on Earth is NOW! This is the only world you will ever know while here! Be sure you have these three principles ingrained in your mind before you begin to explore other realms.

If you do not know where you belong and slip out of one frame into another from time-to-time, you may lose yourself in the maze. You are here for this period of time and are to remain until all your work here is done. At that time you can go back and repeat what you did not do correctly this time—plus additional work, or go ahead to the next area of development, which is on a higher plane.

Apparently the only one who cannot design a life for you is *you*. Too many people run from one person to another seeking help now. You might think they are not in charge of their lives, but they are. You need to learn to think for yourself or you will not be able to advance. You also need to learn to accept responsibility for all of your actions or not advance. However, you cannot play God and attempt to straighten out others' problems for them!

What you need to do and actually do are usually different. You have a long history of life at the top of a heap while here on Earth, but you came here from far below this realm. You need to advance to the next plane and be done with this trial period, but too many prefer instead to linger here and return again and again and again. Work is not better for being put off, so get on with it now!

Whatever you do on Earth is not as interesting as what another is doing in outer space—if your news bulletins are to be believed by us. Why is that? You have a beautiful planet being destroyed by all of you now, because you do not care about it.

You refuse to take precautions to mold your lives into a form adaptable to Earth, yet all expect Earth to adapt and be despoiled by you, so you can all live well now. This is not welcome news to those above. You are viewed as spoiled individuals likely to contaminate the higher realms, unless chastised upon arrival or shortly before.

Put your life on hold, let it smolder and what do you get? Ashes! If you do not raise your level of energy and do your work now, you will receive nothing worthwhile. You cannot catch fire and bring forth a new you or wipe out work that is of no use to you or anyone else. You merely sit and get angry. Anger is your way of reacting when things are not going *your* way.

If you are not determined to be the boss, you do not care how the boss acts. If you are unskilled, you do not care if others are not. If you are happy, you do not mind if others are happy—or not; but if you are sad, you want everyone to be miserable, too.

The old adage that misery loves company is not only of this world, but of others below this one. It means, if you cannot get your own way, you seek misery or demand to be unhappy, which can become your sole source of company. You are unfit for human companionship, but others like you gravitate toward you. We see nothing fun-filled or hopeful about such behavior, and know no others who do either, but many humans continue to enjoy being miserable.

If you cannot control your emotions, why try to intimidate others into acting as you wish them to behave? People often share intimate moments with others, appearing to be enjoying themselves a lot when they are not. They scandalize themselves by rude behavior only to be upset when others do the same. Why? You believe you are special—better than others!

Do not impress upon any child they are special, because it will end in misery for all involved. You cannot let a child grow up believing the world will be a better place simply because of their presence. You cannot let anyone believe they take precedence over all others. Such ideals lead individuals to become vain, pretentious, and bold. This in turn can lead to no friends, misery, and early death. Three fates that grow progressively worse with time.

You will never know who you are if you never sit alone and ponder who you are now. You can sit and dream or sit still and meditate, but you need to always think about why you are here. You also need to desire to be the best you can be at everything you do. You need to keep your life straight and on course and let others do their work.

When a woman becomes a mother, she often thinks of herself as a slave to another person, but she is not. She is the child's rock he or she clings to for the first ten to twelve years, as well as the respected elder who is referred to later whenever crisis strikes that one's life. If a woman cannot enjoy this role of being mother, helper, friend, and advisor, she should not get pregnant!

Pregnancies are argued about on Earth now as if litters of pigs are being cut from a sow so she can breed again, but none of you think much of children! You argue and fight to protect a fetus and then abandon the children as they age. You cannot expect a woman who is totally unprepared for the awesome responsibility of birth and raising a child to be held guilty for not wishing to accept it. If she continues a pregnancy until the child is delivered and then dumps it into another's arms, she is doing the child a disservice.

If you are a mother, you alone are the choice of that soul. You are who was chosen to raise the child. You cannot expect anyone else to do it! You will not be released of your responsibility for this child or be allowed to pretend later in life that the birth never occurred.

When a woman or man is so enamored with another that sex is sought to demonstrate that love, a new life is precious to one or both lovers. If this is not the case, as is so often true now, the by-product of such a union is not wanted. To bring an unwanted child into the world, desert it, and then try again later for another child is not to be condoned. You will raise what you sow and reap the results, or you will be unable to rise above it later.

When responsibility for raising children is handed out by the world, men are often overlooked. Why? This particular world was designed by men—but now being destroyed by women due to a lack of consideration for children. Many men idly stand by watching as women work to rebuild a new world—and they will, but what about the children—where do they fit into this new plan?

If men are to adjust to The World of Tomorrow, they best begin now to accept more responsibility—and eat less. People are not what they eat, but food can ruin an otherwise good life. If your body is unsuited to the work you do, you will have problems. You can adjust the mind to do almost any kind of work, but the body cannot adjust as easily.

If you expect the body to reshape itself in order to conform to your idea of its physical needs, you will become misshapen and disappointed. Please do not remodel your body. Keep your body in great shape and repair it as needed, but do no major alterations to the exterior if you want to live painlessly.

What a doctor does to cure the body is nothing compared to what the body does on any given day, but you revere such men and women as gods now. You need to understand that you are all alike. You are here to do a job, too.

You need to practice and learn a lot before you experiment and develop your style, then deliver excellent service all the days of your life— no different from any other professional human being. Remember, all who work in the world are professional—even bricklayers, quarrymen, and cooks. You are the world and the work you do is for the world—and for *you*.

Whatever you do in this world produces a strain upon your flesh, and your back reacts to it first. If your back is not as limber as it once was, you will be unable to design a new way of life if this one ends abruptly. You need to be on top of everything to know if life is about to take a rude turn and you awaken to another, totally different work. To survive, you need to adapt to new surroundings and work with many different people. Once you can, you have accomplished one of the major works of this life.

When you see people enter your competition's business, do you fear they are rejecting you? Some become so entailed in the operation of another's business that it becomes their business! You are not to do this, even in preparation for a huge transaction. In order to maintain balance, keep your business in its proper place. If your competitiveness begins to operate on you like a business, you will go bankrupt. We are not afraid of bankruptcy, but you are.

Your body can deteriorate, your mind and spirit often do, too, but you fear most losing your money. Why? You are totally attached to it— believe it or not.

Money cannot love, hate, or steal from you, but you think it is the goal of work you must do while here. It is not. Money is never as deep a subject as most would like to believe it to be, but it is not an easy subject to master, either. It requires skill in balancing all assets against liabilities; thus, it resembles *you*. If you master the art of money, you are home free.

The majority see themselves as a series of misadventures and mistakes, but you are more like a patchwork quilt than anything else. You look great from above, but if you look up from below you can see all the knotty problems and stitches that easily come unraveled; thus, you do not think your work to be excellent or beautiful. Try to see things as we do and you will be better for it.

Studying the sky is not the easiest experiment all of you could set out to prove while on Earth, but it was determined it would be the epitome of man's growth, thus you all work to get something going in space while ignoring the space in which you live today. What happens when you ignore what should be taken care of by you in order to pry into others' work—*you* lose!

If you put your life in the hopper and grind it into powder, you achieve either a fine or rough grain. Do you wish to refine it further? It costs more, but does not improve it. In fact, it takes away the features that make it outstanding and different. Keep it in mind before you enroll in a class of any kind. Be sure you want to change. It may take more out of you than it can add.

Education is not the subject of this book, nor is it dominant in any of our works, but we are teachers, so it is always there—just beneath the surface. If you question the authority of our words, you cannot learn from us. When you spend time trying to dominate a spiritual being, you cannot concentrate on what is going on inside your mind.

For example: A student deliberately ignoring a teacher is determined to fail. However, if a student tries to attain the teacher's level of understanding, it is achieved. The mind alone does not study. Spirit is also involved and can do more than either the mind or body can do alone.

Welcome the work of the New Age and begin seeing yourself as a person who is not afraid. **The message for Today is: *You are not to fear!*** If you fear, you cannot be *you*. If you love, you are unable to fear. Love and fear do not dwell in the same mind at the same time. Love is spiritual and fear is of the mind. The mind cannot accept both concepts at the same time. Be sure you love far more than you are loved, so you can more easily change recipients whenever the time comes to do so.

Death and divorce are two types of separation from loved ones that can be totally devastating to one or both parties involved, if no time was spent contemplating the ending of the relationship. You must remember you came alone to Earth and will leave alone—and all others you meet along the way are here for only a short time. If you do not accept this basic belief, you will break down at times when someone leaves you to go on another trail. You must let others lead their lives as you lead your life, or you will be guilty of murdering another's spirit.

In the ending of life are many days when you can sit and stare at the wall. Right? Not if you work every day of this life. You will never have time to merely sit and contemplate the great beliefs of this world. You have to fit your work in as you live.

To us, one day a week spent insuring you are connected to the inner world of YOU is a very short time, but too many of you insist you have no time to do it now. You whine and complain to each other for hours about time, eating up all the time you have crying about it. Why not enjoy yourself, get out in the world enough to see yourself as others see you—then meditate and design a better life? You can accomplish so much more if you sit and relax first. Why wait until your workday is over to meditate? Start out meditating and your day will be filled with energy.

You may or may not enjoy meditating for long periods of time, but the real *you* loves it! You may not sit comfortably enough to keep the body happy, but the soul is thrilled whenever you meditate. When did you pay more attention to *you* than to your mind or body? If not for quite a while, you have a lot of time to make up; but if you meditate and pray daily, not as much time is wasted.

We are not here to study why you are so busy you neglect your life. We are here to find out why you mismanage your '*lives*'—and you do! You sit and do little for an hour, then race about for two. You do not sit and look at the clock in order to time yourselves. Also, we see nothing amusing in the pastime of sitting still to read on the toilet and never reading again the rest of the day. It is not the body's need to gain information, but the mind's need. How can the mind concentrate while the body is in full production?

Think of all you do daily. Do you enjoy doing any of it? Some do *nothing* each day that pleases them. Why? They believe martyrs receive greater rewards at the end of life. Wrong! No one receives anything at the end. It comes to you along the way. If you do not receive a daily blessing, you do not deserve it or are not asking for it. Which is it? You decide.

What you do today is the key to tomorrow's work. If by now you have not done all you came here to do, you can stop anywhere and say: *"I just don't get it."* If you decide to work, start by saying aloud: *"Live and let live. Life is beautiful!"* The difference is: Did you do your work or not? The answer is: Not if life is different for others than what you experience. When your life is predetermined to achieve growth and development, you feel pressure to be different from the rest of your species now. If you are stagnant, no growth is occurring now, but at any moment you can open to full growth.

You have a problem if you dislike the elements. Rain, snow, and sleet are not problems in themselves, rather changes to the Earth. You are here as a temporary resident—not as an owner, and you have to adapt to the elements needed by Earth to exist. If you crave attention, you will learn others are not that interested in you. Why would the Earth care about you if you do not care about it?

These topics are interrelated!

All of life is intertwined and related, but not always in an obvious way or manner. Before you attempt to redirect your life in a different way, why not discover much about you by tracing your roots back to source to determine why you are as you are now.

Think about Earth. Think about your role while here on Earth. Think about why you came here. Think of what it is you came here to do. Think of all you can do to help Earth while here—to repay its hospitality and generosity. That is when you will begin to see the light, regardless of how dark you painted this life.

Imagine a philosopher sitting in front of her word processor... Do you see her writing like an author? Do you see her sitting and carefully choosing each and every word? If you do not see her, you are no philosopher, but can become one. Ask for help contemplating any of the previous thoughts given as necessary to complete your knowledge of Earth and *you* at this time—then take time to think about it.

What if you became a philosopher? What changes would be necessary in your everyday life? None! You do not need physical props to be a philosopher. You only need time alone.

When you sit and contemplate the meaning of YOU, do you? Most likely you sit and think about bills and emergencies you fear you might have soon. If you fear anything, you do not sit and talk much; but if you love much, you may talk too much.

Love is a goal of life!

You have to earn love every day. You cannot be ugly and nasty one day and expect others to always remember you as a charming, wonderful lady or gentleman. The mind too easily forgets the past and accepts the present as being true. Be sure you are the same every day so the impression remaining in everyone's mind is that you are a lady or a gentleman—but do not count on it. People tend to minimize the positive efforts of the rest of humanity while maximizing their puniest efforts.

Hate never helps! Hate destroys love faster than fire can consume dry wood. If you hate, you are hate-filled and unable to grasp the meaning of love. If you ever destroy anyone, you are damaged by it far more than they may be. You will be unable to see why you are damaged, but will sense you are—and know it with certainty later in life.

Most illness stems from some source of hatred, but not to be construed as being responsible for it—rather a by-product of hate. You need to clear your body and mind daily of hate in order to revive your life before you ship it to outer space for storage. You cannot handle much hate! It overcomes the positive wave lengths of energy within you. You have to frequently download energy when in the presence of hate-filled people—so avoid them.

Working in the dark or in the light is no different, except there is a bit of light in any dark place and no dark in any light. Be sure you know which is which!

When you can dance lightly through life, you have learned the secret of success. No one wants you if you trample their dreams. Be of the light—not the dark and life is great! Work for good times to come and they will happen. You have to plan and believe before you can achieve.

This is not the most difficult chapter in this book, but it is the deepest! You will find wisdom is deceptive. The easier something appears to be, the harder it is to achieve.

You will know if work is meant for you or not. When it looks so easy you *just know* you know it, you do not! If you were told or read something that angers you, you were not ready for it; nevertheless, you need to think about it. That is the sum of all you need to know. When you need something, ask and it is there—sooner or later—depending on how important it is to *you* now.

We will end on this note: **You are the only one to be you. Enjoy it and be glad! If you do not enjoy your life, who will?**

Chapter Eleven

The World of Tomorrow exists today! You are the only one in this World of Tomorrow who will know *you*. You must be you today in order to perform in any manner like *you* are tomorrow. If you act like someone else now, tomorrow will set up unrealistic conditions for *you* to continue and complete in order to live there. You need to add to your life each day—not subtract from it.

If you want less in the future than you have here, ask for less now. When you get to the point where you are flooded by answers, problems, or material goods, you need to stop and examine why you asked for so much. You need to sort through it all and wonder why. If you do not come to any clear conclusion, then you have too much and need to pare back until you can handle what you have now. What if you pare back too far? Nonsense, you will never have too little, but you may ask for too much.

Too much work deadens the spirit. Too much money hardens the heart. Too much admiration kills the mind and produces a huge ego. Too much of anything is tough to work with or ignore. You become a slave to its maintenance, and worry it will run out. For the fullest of lives, live frugally and enjoy each and every bit. You never have to worry about having little, if you have enough to eat, a place to sleep, and enough work to keep you busy during the day.

The world insists on creating contests designed to keep everyone active. You play games as a child and continue them all your life, but why? You are not restless beings, but you are lazy. To be inspired to work, you need to be tempted by things that can only be enjoyed *after* you are done with your work.

You are not to plan a life without relaxation and meditation, but most of you do that now. You plan careers, marriages, homes, budgets, bank accounts, and all manner of other activities, but seldom think you need time for *you*. You do!

You should enter your sacred time into the week's activity log first, then the labor. You will always find work to fill in the rest of your time, but labor may not let you find time to be *you*. Why? The ego controls the work area of life, but not *you*—and the ego wants to control *you*!

Your ego is not an evil instrument of 'the devil'. It is not even evil. However, all evil that comes to you is from the ego—yours or others. You will not find evil in the spiritual realm! That is totally incomprehensible. The ego may decide to act spiritual in order to work evil against you or others, but it is still ego—not spiritual in nature.

Ever wonder how your ego could harm *you*? It is very easy! You are easily self-deluded. You are easily harmed by your fear of life and others—which comes straight from your mind. You will not let others enter your life for fear *they* will work evil, while it is you who harms others constantly by excluding them from your life. You also can offer yourself bad advice and believe it is coming from your Higher Self. That is the worst of all self-delusions, because it masks itself as God and is not.

Your spouse is not an enemy, even if you no longer like him or her. You are who changed if you no longer want to be married. Recognize others as they are and deal immediately with changes. If you want to keep your partner or mate, you have to return to whatever role you played during courting, or do a lot of fast talking to win them over to the new role you wish to play now. If you are not changing—as all of life does, you remain in the old days of your marriage and cannot adjust to the present, let alone the future. Why would you lag behind? Fear! Whatever reason you give for no longer being happy in a marriage, it has to do with change. Be sure you know that before you apply for a divorce.

How you do it is more important Than what you do!

That simple adage is repeated, repeated, and repeated, yet few think of it while working. If the final outcome is to be excellent, you need to concentrate on each step of the process. If your daily chores look sloppy, you are not doing them well. You have to do a lot of work to do it right; but if you do each step carefully, the final outcome lasts. If your work stands the test of time on Earth, it is obvious you did a fine job. If your work is easily destroyed or collapses, it was not done well. Be sure your work is representative of *you*—and all you do is good.

Whatever you do, do not permit others to take credit due you or give you undue credit. If you do everything well from its inception and plan properly before you start work on the project, nothing will collapse half-way through the job. *For example:* Without the proper tools and materials, you cannot wash dishes properly and easily. You cannot do anything without planning—simple or complex. Remember how to succeed and you will.

If you decide to have a good time, where you go is not that important. We watch The Scribe shopping. She is determined to get a bargain and always does. Why? She expects it! You cannot get much out of life if you do not expect to achieve it. If you overestimate your capacity for life, you will be disappointed, but you cannot get much more than you have, unless you expect more from time-to-time than you currently possess.

Whatever work you do, do not expect others to worry about it. You should not, either. Instead, do it right the first time. Love doing good work! It may not be the job you have now, but work must fit into your life or you cannot exist here.

Be sure to enjoy the time you have on Earth, and do all you can while here, because you will be gone soon. Once you decide to never work again, your life begins shutting down, and you immediately feel things are going badly here. You cannot end your life, but YOU will.

Even if spiritual work does not interest you now, keep at it if you intend to live well. It is what holds *you* together. What you do here is not important if you do it well, because most people love whatever makes them happy. If you sing, dance, or joke for a living, you will be well paid. If you embalm, butcher, and clean, you are not as well paid, but have total job security and will never need another profession as long as you live here.

Work is not to be derived from others' lives or used to exploit them. If you do, sooner or later you lose all you derived in that manner. Most stock marketing is of this sort of labor, thus not stable, so work in this area at your own risk. If you enjoy helping people amass wealth and gain stability in *their* lives, you will enjoy your labor and amass wealth—and your work (spiritual life) will continue to grow.

Work of a different nature than what you usually do is seldom enjoyed immediately, but may be building strong references you will need in the future. Often an apprentice can handle all of the master's work long before it is known by the world. The master remains the master, so no one prefers a lesser one to handle their needs, but you are wise to help an apprentice, even while seeking the master. If the work is not good, you need a master's touch to correct it; but apprentices learn more from you than their masters if you give them work and help them correct what may not be properly done—before you go to the master about it.

When you need help, you need it then—not later. If you urgently ask for help, we respond. However, if you respond only at times when it is convenient to your schedule, your inner being will not quickly respond to you, either.

We are of You, obviously. You are not of anyone else but God, but some people profess to know God as their personal savior and other blasphemous *'utterings'* meant to denote themselves as being superior to the rest of humankind. Instead, it denotes you as being evil rather than good. You cannot know God! God is. God does not exist to know you.

When you commit blasphemy you wipe out all your work up to that time. *For example:* If you say you can control your fate or destiny, you are in grave danger of wiping out all your work now. Even a silly boast is considered blasphemous if uttered in vain and wantonly destructive ways.

Note that if you boast, you feel strange or funny afterwards. This is caused by an illness you started in your mind. You must be humble to enjoy the good life. If you get too ego-involved while here on Earth, you cannot ascend later.

What you do now is small compared to what you can do or even what you should do, but it still counts, because you are keeping busy. If you are not harming others and are never boastful, you are doing fine now. If you do not feel busy, you are not working hard.

You need to seek the homes and study those who understand the way things act as anchors and how others are barriers to progress. Try to sort out the way they live and compare it to your ways, then copy what is good and ignore what is not.

Models help us all!

We all need to know what is acceptable and what is not. No one else on Earth cares if you never provide a model for others to live by. If you set up unrealistic models of perfection or do not care about it, you will not be inspired to do your best. However, if you set up an ideal that suits you and is good for you to follow—like an ideal parent, you can hold them up as ideals for many years or until you are ready to live on your own.

Adults seldom reach maturity without having good adult models available. If not, they usually have poor social skills. Social skills are lacking today due to the neglect of yesterday's parents. How do you improve them now? Once neglected in childhood, it is extremely difficult, but it can be done. Set up a model to follow and you will correct your most obvious faults.

If you are content to let this life go, you will inspire no one—not even your children. Be realistic, you had an ideal when you arrived on Earth—perhaps lost it, but you can still be a role model. *'Wearing the age of man like a robe'* is not to say you are wise, but it connotes wisdom.

Put on your finest robes and leave them on, unless preparing to labor or go to sleep. To take off your clothes many times during a day indicates you are uncertain about who you are. Clothes are not the stuff of which you are made, but they do reflect who you are. If you change clothes constantly, your *auric* field is brushed aside too often—thus cannot establish itself. You will notice clothing models often become shallow, less interesting than the average person as they age. Why? Their auras are not dense enough to contain the wisdom they need to live a full life. You will also notice this is not true if the model rarely works. Life lifts up rather than removes *auric* waves. It is you who removes or damages that field!

To brush up on your character references, you need to talk. If you hear nonsense coming through your lips, you are not studying others enough. If you talk in riddles, you are not listening enough. If you are unhappy, others shy away from you. If you are rude, few talk to you civilly. But if you are loved, all stand close to you, hug you, or smile as you talk.

Do not let life deceive you, Examine your life daily!

When you sit down to eat, it is for the body and soul. You are not mentally involved. You may decide what to eat, but that is about all the mind does then. When you start eating, your soul appears—and you enjoy the process or not. Be sure to enjoy all you eat or it becomes so heavy it cannot leave and will increase the size of your body—not *you*.

We cannot eat, but we require energy, too. You require energy for your body which you get from food. You also require the same energy we use to survive in this world. Spiritual energies are all around you here, but food is not. You have to strive to keep food entering the body daily, but no effort is required to absorb universal energies.

Wearing clothing that restricts the body is unwise. If your belt is too tight, you end up with gut problems. If your back is restricted in movement, it becomes weak. Big, wide belts to help avoid accidents weaken more backs and hurt more people later in life than they help now, but man is constantly told to use such things because greed in the present supersedes wisdom of use to the future.

Work to alleviate pain and suffering within you and you reduce it in all who are around you now. Your pain enters the airways and can hit others. It is felt by *The Healers*! It is never the same, but pain can be felt by children or parents when one or the other ails. You have to protect yourself against the undue attacks of others' ills by respecting their pain and giving back love. This flow of energy often heals others.

We are unable to share all we know with you, since you are not ready for it, but when you are, teachers are always ready to help. However, you have to seek! You have to study and work! Study is not the same as labor, because it immediately enriches you, while you labor for the future—not the other way around as you may think now.

Worms are squashed by earth. They live, breathe, and eat within it and keep on multiplying, but seldom survive long above ground. You live on Earth and breathe its oxygen and eat foods you gather there, but cannot survive far above it without manipulation of your airways. You are no different than worms!

When you believe you are better than any other creature on Earth, you act with distinct displeasure. You treat whomever or whatever viciously and with hurtful cruelty. If you awaken to each creature's respect for nature, you may see each creature is much like what you seem to be.

Fishing the seas in order to eat all that is there is not being a friend to the animals on Earth. Do not spare one to eat the other as is done now. You can raise enough of one to spare the other, and eat enough of one so as not to deplete too many of the other. Think and be sensible with the resources of Earth—and work with it.

Farming is outrageously overpriced by those who make it a business. If you love to farm, all will come to you for produce and crops you grow, but you will not have huge surpluses. Why produce more than you need? It can become a burden and sadden you if the harvest goes down in size—no longer feeling satisfied with just having enough. It is not wise to increase your wants in order to have more of what you need!

Why not farm (garden) for just enough to feed you and your loved ones? It is too time consuming—or so you say. What are you doing instead? Are you instead watching television, sitting around fighting with your family, or acting the fool for others? You need to be busy—and keeping your family fed is the best of all activities.

You may not be able to raise food, but you can cook it. If you never cook, your food is seldom done exactly as you want it. If you eat others' food, you eat what they like or complain and upset your stomach. No bitterness or emotional upset should accompany any meal. If it does, the stomach hurts and the body does not properly absorb food. Illness comes to those not careful about what they eat.

"Work now, for the day is short," is not an idle statement. Your days on Earth are short, because you are not to linger here. Begin to accept what you must do immediately before leaving Earth, and do it first. Whatever you need done secondly is of little importance, because you most likely never get to it. There is only enough time to do what needs to be done first.

Walking about on two legs is not a talent, but dancing is. You cannot do anything about your legs if they do not want to dance. They will not dance on their own. Your mind is not able to force the feet to dance, but Spirit can. Spirit is the energizer of all *you* are and can change the nature of all things—good and bad.

Your nature is not natural!

You decide each day how you live—and why. You decide where you will go and when. You decide if you are happy or sad. If set on your spiritual path, you will not let others hurt or destroy you. If mentally or physically wandering about from place-to-place looking for *something*, you will be beset by villains who easily spot the flickering of your inner light.

You are an electrical being that produces a large volume of sound and light. If you do not connect well to your source, you flicker or produce static, which brings out the worst in all around you. You need to be strong enough to withstand attack. Respond with alarm and shriek if such attack catches you by surprise. You need to always be able to react swiftly. Do not let anyone attack you! Make sure they know you will react.

What you need now is not another lesson, but a chance to absorb all we have told you in this chapter. Let it sink into and enter your mind now—even though it is already within *you*. Spirit absorbs at a high rate what the mind cannot see. Your body responds only to the urgency of the mind—otherwise, it does its own job in its own way.

You are the spirit of this mind and body. You (the Higher Self) are in charge now. Live that way today!

Chapter Twelve

The only people unable to become whomever they are meant to be are those totally preoccupied with self now. You cannot be *you*, if you see no one but yourself. Why?

The entire World of Tomorrow is based on Today. If you are not a part of Today's World, how can you fit into The World of Tomorrow? Keep in mind you cannot fit in any better than you do now. You decide if your life is better or worse than it was yesterday. If it is better, you are living in a positive mode. If it is not better, you are not.

Life is not about living each day as though it were your last, but living in that mindset does help you stay focused on Today. Decide what will keep you focused and use whatever it takes to keep on top of life—not fall behind. If you lag behind the crowd now, you usually settle for second-best or whatever is left. If you walk to the front to take your place there, you can find a better spot than you are in now.

Those upset today are not doing their best work here and now. *You* do not like it if you do not help yourself. You will be upset if you cannot see yourself improving or achieving more each day. It is unwise to compare yourself to others, since they do not have your goals in life; however, you should constantly compare yourself to *you*.

YOU is a word we use to describe the essence of You (your Higher Self), in other words, your soul. In so many ways, *you* are not a complete soul while on Earth. You are here to learn, develop, and enjoy what is provided, but you cannot do everything you will do once reunited with all that is You (the Higher Self).

While here on Earth you need to understand that You is not here. If you feel yourself melding into the work *you* does, you are then You! It is easy to be you, if you know who you are—or at least know that part of *you* that is here on Earth; but you cannot expect others to know who you are. The egotism of man is to believe others should care more than you care for *you* or anyone else.

Put your heart on a table and see if *you* exist there. No, you do not reside in your heart, liver, or pancreas—all of which make up the major organic work of the body. You are the unique being within the body— and there to do a job. *You* came here to work, then leave for the next level or plane, but some become so engrossed in the mechanics of this world that they never want to leave Earth. This is happening now! That is why many are being told to get on with their work now and be ready to leave Earth at the end of this life—so others can finish their work here, too.

What you do or what you say has little to do with who *you* are, if you are out of touch with the reality of *you*. If you believe all you see is all there is, you have no idea who *you* is. You cannot be all you are if you were never *you*. Until you realize *you* are involved, too, you cannot wonder at the enormity of the world's preoccupation with self and its total ignorance of what is.

Why would anyone choose Earth now, If they could live anywhere?

This world is an assignment that challenges most souls, therefore, is sought out by many intent on being all they can possibly be, but it is not the pleasantest place to live now. You have nothing to compare to life elsewhere, because those memories are erased before you enter this atmosphere and will not be returned until you leave Earth.

Where you are now is of little consequence if you cannot leave Earth when the time comes to go. You can be here or there and still die or enter a coma. You can be at home or away and still decide you will not ascend. We want you to be ready for death—wherever you are, so you can travel or sit, knowing you are ready to cross over and can ascend to a better life within your soul.

While here on Earth, many form silly, superstitious ideas about the old ways, where you came from, and what lies ahead of you now. These ideas are not based on truth or reality, yet you believe them and prevent yourself from advancing while here on Earth. Why? You do not want to leave this world! You want to stay here until Earth is no more. Since you do not want to go beyond the limitations of this world, you hold *you* back!

Where you are now in the world is of little use to *you* once you leave—while here it presents a measuring stick of sorts. You can see how much you learned while here or you can ignore others. You can see how well others are doing compared to the roles they cut out for themselves, and you can create a campaign to reelect you to stay in this world. Why would you want this world to continue? You might believe it is the only one like it.

You cannot expect people to be with you at the end of your life if you ignored them all this life—can you? Well, some believe God will be waiting with open arms on the final day and you will walk right in and be welcomed then. What a surprise you have waiting for you!

Work is done daily—not in stages or episodes—but in daily increments. If you do nothing that benefits you or the world, you are doing nothing now that counts then. You might as well be in a cell with no air or water, since you are dying, not growing.

What the world needs now is not love, but the spiritual work of those who love. You cannot expect an emotion to do much. The hands work, the mind thinks, arms hold, eyes see, but love does nothing. The world needs much work now. Get busy!

Where *you* are now, and why *you* are here, is never of great interest to others around you now. You may believe people are interested in your travels, but try to see it as they do. They do not believe what they cannot see—and neither can you. It is difficult to believe in an unseen, over-all Lord of the Universe if you feel nothing, see nothing, and never heard of the presence of such a being while here.

Since so many today live in places where all knowledge of the past has been erased—and you do not talk about God for fear of your fellow man, you do not know who *you* are or where you are going, thus you are afraid to be yourself every day. You need never fear the dark again or fear being alone! By believing in God you can erase all fear from your life—or continue as is.

You decide where your faith is—God or man. If you believe only in God, you are never alone. If you believe man is the ruler of the universe, you are always alone.

Over the years of an average lifespan many are unable to say they are of God. Why? They do not believe God exists—or fear God may not exist. Decide early, then stick by your original decision to see where you are at the end of this life once you decide to return and make up for any lost time, or go forward to the next plane where life is growing and all is well within *you*.

Worry is of man—not God! If seeking perfection within your work, you need to worry at times, but worrying over the facts of life is unacceptable. Notice that great people worry over big decisions and are usually not bothered with commonplace matters. Why? If you think big, you have only so much energy and cannot easily tailor it doing small things.

Think big now!

Whatever you do in this life, it is for *you*—not for someone else. Regardless of what others say, they do all they can to help themselves, too. You are not the only one on Earth, but the only one responsible for you. If you let others take what is yours to enhance their lives, you are committing a sin against yourself. If you struggle, we will help you eliminate those who oppress you, but be sure you are free before asking for freedom.

Freedom is not a gift of democracy, but democracy is the best environment to foster freedom now. You can see in every democracy those who are not truly free, they prefer to be told what to think or do. Enter any demagogic society and you find those who are free, but not enjoying any freedom within their world. Freedom is a matter of mind—not body. You decide you are free and you are!

Whatever you do to the life you have now is not nearly as important as what this life does to *you*. You will not know it is the end of this world until it happens, even though you are who ends your world here. You are the world you see now!

Wherever you go on Earth, it is always the same. You never change from one time to another or from one place to another. Thus, it is never wise to travel until you can be all you are every place you visit, then you can be you and enjoy all you are there to do—and later not remember only bad things you saw or what went wrong.

What a child does is not bad, but how the adult perceives it is. You may not realize at heart how bad you are now until you see a child doing much the same as you did at the same age. You may not realize how great you are until you see a child accused of being bad when that is what made you who you are today; but to let bad behavior go, because it did not harm you as a young person is always unwise.

Wisdom is needed when you help others grow and mature. You need to use all you have and think you have to help another grow beyond their life of being a toddler, misfit, or teenager, before they can live well on their own. If you sit and let them struggle, you help them more than those who sincerely try to eliminate all pain and suffering from children's lives. It takes wisdom to know when it helps and when it harms you or another to give assistance or accept help.

What you do now is not as important as what you will do when you are at the end of this life and need to move on. If your life's bank account is overdrawn then, you discover perhaps too late that you are not ready to ascend. You need to save and put away something for that time.

Money is not the economy of the universe, but money is the method used on Earth to ease you into the salvation of your soul. If you know how to handle money while on Earth, you are half-way home at the end of this life. If you are greedy, steal from others, ignore the needs of those not ready for this life, or you do not know how to live within your means now, you will be bankrupt at death, too.

Worry over money is the number one prayer on the lips of all who pray today. Why? You have made money your god! You pray as though money will answer all your problems and put you on top of this world. You sorely misunderstand what money represents.

Work is usually paid for with money, but more and more do not use it. Why? They can see it only as a medium of exchange needed to obtain goods for services. You can also trade goods or services without money. However, you cannot do such things correctly if you do not understand money.

Whatever you do now, you do it to earn a living, educate yourself, or relax. If you cannot do any of these without money, you are in big trouble, because no one earns enough to satisfy all these desires. Today's mentality is: You do not need money to make a living. You simply work at making a living. You can get a loan or sacrifice to pay for things if you do not have them. You do not need money to educate yourself, and you do not need money to entertain others.

'Work' is a difficult word to understand, if you constantly avoid the issue. Your life is defined more or less by your career or lack of one while on Earth, and you must wonder if this is the correct way to think now. It is. You know instinctively that work is important to *you*. It is not to be shunned or overridden by those who do nothing but supervise others. Your work is not to be derided if you do what is necessary— particularly if you are ordered to do it for the common good. You will never be upset by those who appreciate your work.

When you do not understand the nature of activity, you will believe all work is unpleasant—which is false! When you do what has to be done, that is work. When you do what you want to do, that is fun. If you have much to do and do not do it, you are lazy. On the other hand, if you have a lot you could do, but do not need to do it, you are not lazy.

Why be lazy? It is your way of avoiding life here and now. Life is not here and now, but always! You cannot avoid it. You can delay your advancement—but not end it or avoid the consequences of your behavior. You can grow only as far as you let yourself grow. If you stop to look at you every day or so, you may not see anything change. So do not stop and stare daily at all you are or all you do, instead rest, relax, and do all you can—then check it out.

What if you relax and no one else does? It might look as if you are lazy, but if your work is up-to-date, you are not lazy. Your life may look like a breeze to others, but everyone's life is difficult *for them*. Your life is your design, and originally it was not influenced by anyone else. However, you often choose to adopt other peoples' lifestyles or patterns of living as you go through life, because they intrigue you or you believe they are better than what you do. However, if you do not know who you are, it seldom proves to be true for you.

Work on the basics first!

Decide who you are this life and where you are going before asking others for help. If you ask and no help presents itself, you are not on the right path for you, or you do not need help. Perhaps it is then time to ask for redirection or ask for help deciding on a new path—all is available, just ask!

When you can clearly see yourself as you are now and act accordingly, others may say you have changed. You have not! You are being true to *you*. When you cannot understand life and why you are here, and on-and-on, you are lost and need help, but only *you* can know that. For assistance, wait until you can be alone for a time, then pray for help and guidance. Whoever is listening then will help you.

When humans decide to call for help today, they often go straight to angels. Why? They are afraid of all other beings. Why? They were never told they have Spiritual Guides, or that other spiritual beings will help them. Why? Churches were reluctant in the past to let people respect themselves as being of God and knowing what to do with their own lives. They fostered an atmosphere of doubt and fear in order to control access to the higher planes. You do not see anything quite like it now, but many still fear *The Church* remains that way and will inhibit their individual calls to God. Please check out churches before you repeat nonsensical ideas about any of them.

The only one who knows who you are and cares is *you*, but there are others also concerned about you. Your mother and father have a vested interest in seeing you rise beyond this plane, because they are held accountable for your earthly initiation. Obviously, any spouse is interested in your advancement on Earth, but perhaps not above it, because of their connection to personal interests and merging lives here. If you do not do what you came here to do, no spouse can be held responsible for your life!

Where or when you are ready for love is of no concern to others, but you may believe many are interested in your affairs. This is not a problem unless it costs you friends. Friends are not to be overburdened with silly, little worries. You have to learn to handle small things yourself.

If going through a major life crisis alone, you need only concentrate on finding your way, unless someone asks you for help finding their way. If you are on the path and a major life crisis strikes, it is not as bad as it might be—and you can help others then, too. Which circumstance describes you well now?

What people see in others is not a reflection of themselves as much as their need to see it. You do not need to see others to know who you are, but you need to believe others are like you. If no one else believes like you do, you feel uncomfortable. To be of use to others strengthens you, but can also rip you apart. Be sure you are strong enough to help, before you attempt to do so.

What you are now is the real *you* today. You cannot say: *"I will only do this now.'* That is not true. What you do now is today, tomorrow, and forever.

Whenever you work, do it well and let it go. Do not pick at it over and over again or ask others to judge it. You know what is good, and you know that you know, so let it go and move on.

Wherever you work you need time to get there. If it is too hard to get there on time, you need a new job. Why you work is not as difficult for us to understand as the way you do it. As teachers we often see the results of poor work and how it affects every aspect of your personality. Why let poor work change you? Sit and do your work first—relax later.

Do not relax totally as you work!

The only way to be sure your work does not upset others is to ask if you are interfering in any way with them. If you are, ask them to help you adjust. If they help you—adjust. If they do not respond, continue as before, because you obviously are not bothering them then.

There are several different methods available to handle this world's work, as well as the work you must complete to build The World of Tomorrow; however, they cannot be explained in words. Such methods have to be experienced. If you wish to use our help, you have to exist on this plane, yet understand the workings of the higher planes. We cannot help you do this now, but you can learn when this class is over.

The classroom of life is this life. You will not be expected to develop an entire episode of life in a single day, but several days may be all you need. On the day you finally get it all together, you may end all your lives or may decide to go on and more fully explore life here. It is your decision to make.

Once your work here is done, Tomorrow is there. You can see this is not the same discussion as in our previous Book of Wisdom dedicated to the subject of Work, but much rings true as if it were. Why? It is truth! You must work all the time you are on Earth or you will return to do it. In the end of this world's time you will still be here. You may not be here in flesh, but you leave an *auric* ring in this world and may be able to return to it—or not.

What does it take to turn the page and leave another hanging in suspense? Think on this: While you are on Earth, we cannot initiate you into a higher realm, but you can stretch to attain it now. We end this chapter in order to go forward with another—and congratulate you now!

Chapter **Thirteen**

The only tomorrow you will ever see is when you go beyond this plane into the next one—only then are you in The World of Tomorrow. Until then, tomorrow is just a word you use to say: *'never been there—but soon.'*

We want you to concentrate on Today, so when Tomorrow arrives you are ready for it! What you do now is in preparation for that time, yet does not interfere with your present life on Earth—rather enhances it. Why not be all you can be while here?

This is your time to be free of worry and fear, but all here are filled with both emotions. What could possibly be so fearful on Earth? There are no things yet to be discovered or unknown to any of you, except to those most remote who have no access to the outside world. They fear no one here.

You need to reevaluate your mindset now and decide if it is obsolete. Obsolescence is not the worst thing to happen, but it is if you do not regroup. You need to refurnish your mind as often as you would a lovely home. If you let things accumulate before throwing them out, you probably do the same with your thoughts. If you pitch things before deciding if they are workable elsewhere, you do the same with ideas. You within are much like the worker you are in *'real life.'*

The only one who cannot help you out of this dilemma is the one who created you, but you cannot go back. You have to go forward, which means you have to advance. Work while on the way up so it is not as difficult to find a handhold when you fall. Slide up the rail using others' work and you will fall far, far behind if you ever slip. There are many who spiritually try to ride on the shoulders of others' work, and often get fairly far along before being dumped, but they are dumped!

You need to do *your* work! If you sit and dream of times when you could meditate for only two minutes—three at most, you can see how difficult it was then, but now may not think of it as difficult. Try meditating now for two to three minutes....

Did you meditate or did you cheat and skip ahead? If you are the type who easily follows instructions, you meditated immediately and feel great now. If you are the type who likes to see where something is headed before heeding the words of others, you may possibly meditate now, but most will not meditate!

That is how your world is today! You do not need to participate in endless experiments to know that of the seven sins touted as being deadly, sloth is the world's worst sin now. You are lazy if you cannot meditate for even two minutes!

Only now do some realize you are lazy. Instead of meditating, you drifted off, while others meditated. Why? Believe it or not, that is how your mother manipulated you as a child....

If you still react to life in the ways of a child, you cannot address adult issues effectively. You must grow up or die! You must learn to be you, but cannot until such time as you are on your own and independent of others. If you stay within the parental home for many years, you are not independent and are likely to be quite confused as to whom you really are, too.

What you need do to gain access to the work of this world is study. By this time it is all written down somewhere in a book, even though you expect new books will hint at things far greater than already known. You hope that is true, so you have a reason for avoiding reading books of wisdom, but the reason you do not read now is you cannot do so easily.

You do *only* what you do well now. If you cannot read well, you do not read. Some claim they graduated from college, but never read books now. How they graduated from college is not as easy to understand as why they no longer read books. You cannot skip over text in assigned books and graduate. Skipping text in novels, you lose the thread of the plot. With scientific material you cannot come to accurate conclusions.

If you enjoy reading, you just do it! If you cannot read, or have great difficulty reading, you seldom practice enough to read faster. We write in this fashion to appeal to the average American reader who is not adept. If we wrote in convoluted construction and used high-minded terms, most readers today would not follow this text to the end.

If you believe the terms we use are too easy to be wise, you obviously cannot understand what you are reading. If that is true, you need to go back to the beginning of The Books of Wisdom and find where you fell away from the truth. The same is true of life.

Work on this:
   "I am unable to enjoy life, because I am not me."

Now work on this:
   "I am not me, because I love another."

"I love another" is a phrase that does not convey much. It is simply a declaration indicating total lack of self-esteem. You cannot love someone else instead of you. You have to love you first.

It is impossible to circumnavigate the globe and not know where your home base is and how to find it. While discovering this world, many often learn who they really are—What about you?

Work on this: *"I am not afraid!"*
Now work on this: *"I am not afraid of me."*

The latter phrase is one which betrays all. Everyone here is afraid of what they might do in a rough situation or when not prepared. That is why death is so scary to you all now.

If you are so afraid of death now that you wish to totally avoid discussing it, you will never learn it is just another day in this life. You have many days this life—and one will be the last day. Simple to understand, but difficult to accept.

Move your head back and forth, then place it in your hands. Did you place your head in your hands or put your hands up to your head? If you did not follow these directions, you cannot understand how the world works now.

If your present life is confused and uncertain, you probably lost your way. If you never read directions or cannot read well, you will find it very difficult to get beyond the second level of the Earth plane. Others may help you through the first two levels, but at that point it becomes increasingly difficult for all to help others.

Start doing *your* work now! If you cannot read—or refuse to read, you are relying on others too much. Do you really want to be that dependent? If others make all judgments for you, you will never know if you are right or wrong. Why be afraid to know whatever?

When *you* die, you end this life and go forward, but you do not know where you go then. This makes 'the end' appear to be mysterious and dark, but it is anything but dark. It is the brightest hour of this life. You merge once again—even if merely for a brief moment—with the God which is all of us. You cannot end any other way. You decide the end of your life, but you may not stay there long.

When you are elevated to the final level of the Earth plane, you are not dealing with everyday issues of life. You are making the rounds of your mind and people you know, in order to see what you can learn while still here. You try to develop some sense of what is next. You can learn much from previous lives, but you do not use such material. You likely ignore such past work in favor of new work, because this is the way to advance.

If you require much attention, you cannot advance any higher on this plane than Level Three. You must be able to do your work and ignore criticism, even worse—public accolades. If your loved ones are unhappy with your behavior, you may be off the path. Seldom do those who truly love you wish to hold you back. Although it happens in the lower planes, you learn to routinely walk away from such fetters in order to advance.

You may not realize *'the ages of man'* are not levels of this plane, instead correspond to the development of *The Holy Spirit* within man. Also, you may not be aware *'the ages of man'* are merely levels of this Earthly existence. The levels of this plane measure levels of the soul's progress here. It takes time to learn all these things.

Do you want to progress?

You never have time to do anything if your idea of time is warped and distorted. You usually sit and do nothing with your time. You look at work and declare it will not be done. Why? You say, *"I do not have time, or this is the work of an idiot."* The nail is in their shoe then and they cannot travel further.

Some seek channels to do their work. All goes well as long as they hear only good or positive things about themselves. The day they are told they are not on the path or not doing what is right to do now, they declare the channel is no good. Why? It hurts when you are nailed!

Why use a channel?

You do need help deciphering your egoistic line of reasoning from time-to-time, but you do not need a channel to do that. If you have a friend also seeking the light, you can discuss it or not. If you have no one to talk to about spiritual work, a channel who is a light healer can help you. Of course, you have to do your work with Spirit!

When you cannot do your work, you often refer to those who do such work as *dullards, nerds, idiots,* and other nasty words in order to hide your jealousy. Light workers are not nasty. They survive—will you?

Think of all the words you use to put yourself down. Do you say them aloud? If so, you must erase them! Now is the best time to begin.

Now think of a time when you did something stupid. What did you say aloud then? Think about all the other times you committed errors of judgment....

How often do you speak evil of yourself during a day? *'Seldom'*, you say. If true, it is rare, but can be achieved. Never again speak of what you do in a derisive way or tone of voice.

You create the tapes playing in your mind. To erase a faulty or bad tape, simply record over whatever is on it now. Some areas become fuzzy or do not connect properly if erased a lot. The best way to correct ideas is to erase the entire tape, then record a new message. Here is how you can produce helpful tapes correctly and easily:

Begin Each Day With the Following Ritual:
Envision screwing your head on straight, saying aloud:
I am not stupid, dumb, idiotic, or without sense.
I am here to do only good.
I am good!

This easy exercise uses simple words to erase a lifetime of negative background *'noise'* playing nonstop in your mind to accompany your life. Make sure you know what you are playing in your mind now, and when you use it, so you can broadcast the true work of your life to this world. To do it is easy! You are broadcasting right now. To change the channel is difficult only if you do not know how to do it, but you now know, so do it!

What if you do not do what we said? Did you refuse because we made a demand of you? Did you refuse because you do not have time to do it now? Did you refuse merely to be contrary—hate doing what others would do? All of these reasons define fools—not logic. No wise person automatically gives the same response.

Words can make you stop and think, but actions automatically stop your movement. Why? You may not listen or read words closely, but an action occurring in front of you cannot be ignored. You have to respond or not. You cannot continue without answering it then.

No matter where you seek learning, you go to a school or teachers who are the best for you and available at that time, regardless of whether or not it is the school you wished to enter. They are not just there. They are there when you are there to merge with them. If you do not like your school or teachers, you must change them.

What to do if your child is not liked enough by a teacher? Let it go. You teach your child nothing if you do not let him or her learn to deal with those in power, as well as those who do not like them.

These are basic facts of life: You may find leaders who will agree with you, but more likely, you will not. You still need to follow their lead or get new leaders immediately.

When you enjoy the road to poverty, and most who remain poor do, they know no other term to use but: *"I'm poor."* If you do not enjoy being poor, you say: *"I have no money."* There is a distinct difference in what is being said! If you need money, you can ask for it. If you view yourself as poor, you have nothing, because you cannot decide what you need now or how to ask for help effectively.

Whatever you do, you need to ask for help *before* you move forward or seek wisdom. To learn such lessons is not always the easiest move, but you move if you do. You can learn by reading or studying others' behavior, but actually doing whatever by yourself teaches best. It takes a long life to live each and every lesson individually, but if you study and observe others at least some of the time, doing what you wish the rest of the time, life may be briefer, but you do everything you came here to do.

If you need only a brush-up course on life, you will be here for a relatively short time. If you need an entire life rerun, you will stay a longer time. Regardless of when you arrive or leave Earth, you stay until your work here is done.

It is your choice where your reading takes you now. If you are still in school or studying under a teacher, you may be directed to the best books, but someone had to read everything to find the best work. Why spare time to read everything you can? If you intend to teach others, you know you need to know as much pertinent material as possible.

Many teachers are not prepared to do their work when they arrive at a class, but shortly learn what to do. How? They are told what to do. They are shown how to begin and end a series of lessons. They are given books and papers which explain how to do it well. They follow directions! You must know how to learn in order to teach others.

What you do now is of no consequence to us, but you will be considered stupid if you do not do any work. You can see it is not difficult to follow the words of another, but not easy either—especially when it comes from someone who knows more than you.

If you intend to grow, it is necessary to listen and follow instructions. We will never teach you anything, but you can learn from us. When you learn, you do nothing much more than listen or read—Right?

Why not learn to listen well now,
And read even better?

This life is one in which many profess to be teachers. You cannot boast of this! You cannot know if you are a teacher until a student comes forth and says she is your student, or he says he learned something from you. All others are merely sitting in attendance and speaking of what they know.

Where you go and who you know is of no interest to anyone but you. Do you boast of your school? Do you complain about it? It matters not what college or elementary school you attend or attended at one time. It is all about how much you learned while there. You may not see it as much, but there is a big difference between students, but not between schools.

You learn better and faster if the class is equal in number to the seats in the classroom—other than that you cannot complain much. All who start out working together and continue can judge each other's performance best, arriving at similar conclusions more easily, but may not tolerate others well. If you always stay with only those who are like you, you often become clannish and do not allow differences to surface —but you learn faster that way.

When you know your life story is almost over, you may decide to rewrite major portions of it. Why? For the same reason you are where you are now. It is not embarrassing to have had no parents to raise you, or to not have lived in a large home, or you were always awkward around others; but it is embarrassing when you do not read or write well, you cannot remember the name of someone who mattered to you a lot at some time in your life, or you cannot do simple chores for yourself. These are the measures of a full life—not the simple touches that made *you* you.

By the time you get to the next chapter, you will know more than you do now. How is that? It just happens! You read, you study, and you develop as you think. If you do not read, study, or develop, you are effectively dead.

You may not believe you can read, but you can. You may say you cannot study, but you do. Be honest, you know everyone around you and why they are there. If that is not reading and studying life, what is?

We have urged you to read yet another page, but how do you know when to stop working? You run out of energy. You decide you are bored and cannot go on, or you do not have any more time to read now.

What is it you plan to do next? Do you plan to continue your work? Good! Do you plan to sleep instead of read? Good. Do you plan to pray and meditate? Great! If you do that before you do anything else, you grow in God.

Your life will end as it began. You will be alone. No one else can make the journey at the end with you—only *you* will be there. But you can go forward now fully prepared for the adventure—Get Ready!

Chapter Fourteen

This is the new you! Do you believe it? You do not? Then *you* are not accepting who you are. Every second of every minute, hour, and day, you are new. However, you no longer exist once the moment is gone. Time continues as you do—but not beyond this moment.

If you prepare for the future and it does not appear, what happened? You wasted a lot of time! If you waste time, do you feel guilty about it? Most people do. In fact, most people feel, deep within, that there is no time to waste and often wonder why they feel like that here and now. If you are always busy, you do not have to feel guilty.

What if you did all you had to do and there was still a lot left undone? Would you die? The answer is No. If you have a lot to do and never do it, what happens? You have to do it later. What if you came to Earth to do many difficult things and only do a few of them, what happens then? If your future depends upon what you do now, you have to work steadily every day to get it all done before the day ends. If the future depends on you enjoying yourself and earning your own way, what will you do when time runs out?

You will not run out of time! No one ever runs out of time. You may not finish your work, but you had enough time to do it. You cannot alibi out of living your life by saying you do not have time. That excuse is not believed by *anyone!*

What if you do not know what to do or do not know how long you have to do it? Pray for help! Ask for guidance. Decide to get onto the path leading to your final destination and go for it now. When you do that, you discover others help you. People share what they know. If you never help others or share, you may wonder why others would help you, but it happens.

Where you are now is not important. At the end of your life, it is important. If you do little now, you will not be very far along your path when life ends. If you sit and stare at the door, wondering who could be knocking, you waste time. Get up, answer the knock, and see for yourself. If you always do such things, you will not progress, even if you do get beyond this plane—which would be very doubtful.

You are on Earth to become the biggest aspect *you* can be within your entire system, without disintegrating into many different factions. If you cannot stretch or bend, you will break and let everything go, so be able to always work on one thing long enough—to stretch your life. If you drop everything because it is difficult for you to do, *you* will be dwarfed over time by your laziness. Be aware you are who decided to give up on *you*—not another. If you stick to your work, giving it your best, you win. If you work only part-way and then walk away, you lose.

This is the time in life when you can now end up in the driver's seat. However, if you keep looking over your shoulder and behind you, you cannot drive your life forward. To be so involved in yesterday that tomorrow never appears slows your work here.

Work on today and everything is fine!

When you can see into the soul of another, do you look? No, you are never aware you are looking into the heart or soul of another, even when you are. The other person may be aware they are baring a part of themselves so it receives light, but you will be unaware of it. Why? It is too sacred for you to comprehend! You are unfit to look directly upon a soul here.

Art is an expression of the human condition within the soul. It is not a reflection of the soul. You can look at a painting or sculpture and identify the master's touch, but cannot say it is unique because it is done in a media used by many others, or the subject is too familiar, or you recognize the model immediately, or any one of a hundred million reasons why it resembles another picture or sculpture. If you saw the artist's soul, you could not relate to it, because there are no two alike. What you need to do now to get ready for the future is look at you and think…

Why am I different?
Why am I loved by the universe?
Why do I deserve to be here?

These questions are not deep, but you are! You now can see you do not think much. You ponder and wonder, but seldom actually do the hard work of thinking a lot. Why? You say you do not have enough time.

If you hired a man to paint your portrait, would you expect a similarity to exist between your mirror image and his picture of you when completed? Probably! If it did not meet your expectations, you most likely would not pay for the picture you commissioned. Why would you expect this man to be able to paint your picture when you are totally unlike all other living organisms? You think you are like all others!

When you first visit Earth, you think you look quite different from others here, but after a lifetime you begin to settle down and see you look quite the same as everyone else. Why are you unsure of it in the beginning—even going out of your way to look like others? You are not comfortable here, because you are not of Earth. You feel like an alien!

All of you are aliens!

Let us see if you can become foreign in your land now. Buy a home in a neighborhood that is far below your income level and watch how your peers show you little or no respect. Buy a home in a neighborhood quite far from where you live now and people there will ignore you. Build a house in a new development where all moving in are of different ethnic and racial characteristics and you believe you do not fit in—but you do. What makes the difference? In one instance you thought you were the same as everyone else, in one you thought you would be the same, and in another you were all regarded as aliens (strangers).

What if you decide to move to a state where everyone else was the same religion or political party—and you differ from them? What do you think will happen to you? We know! You would change and become more and more like they are now, but they most likely would never notice you had changed.

What if you join a club which requires you to drop all other affiliations in order to belong only to this group, would you do what they demand? If you do, you lose your identity. You become a cog within a gear that circulates the same dogma over and over again so one person may gain while everyone else loses. It is not the way of this world to condemn anything, but this is one practice that should not continue, since it harms all concerned. Think for yourself or risk becoming the tool of someone who thinks for you. Neither tactic is extremely helpful in learning to tolerate all others, but if you do your thing, you do grow.

Where you sit on a bus is not the issue. The problem is: Where is the bus going? To catch the right bus, you need to know its final destination. All buses while in service go somewhere, but only a few run where you want to go. Once you know where you want to go, follow the signs along the way!

If your life is one of idleness and intolerance, you can be sure it will not take you very far and you will eventually be left behind by all. You will be of no interest to others because you cannot help them—and might even expect them to help you. Popularity does not come easily to those seeking help.

Your life is one of people, places, animals, things, and behavior. Which of these will get you what you want now? Behavior! You must be sociable, because no one will do it for you. You have to control your life, because no one else can.

If you sit and stand according to rote all day, you discover you did not conform to the normal practice of others, but you performed. If you sit while others stand and vice versa, you are no different—just not conforming to their routine. This is no big deal, but many get upset if others do not conform to their ideas. Why?

You hate to conform, but you do. You hate to tolerate behavior not conforming to what is expected, but you do it, too. In other words, you hate people who at times do not conform. Instead, be ready for it. Do not get upset by it. Live your life knowing at times you, too, will not conform.

Why would you think others want the same ideals you seek? Your ego is the reason. You want others to want what you want, but cannot see it is not you they seek to be like. People want to be happy. If you are happy, they like you. If you are unhappy, generally they avoid you. It is no big deal! You do the same.

What if you look up and see the moon and stars colliding with each other? You are definitely not in sync then. They are not about to lose their sense of direction, but you often do. Why would you believe others lose their senses?

The ego prefers to believe it is the greatest of all creations, rather than conform to the demands of this life. Why? Because it is not of You (the Higher Self). The ego is a mechanism designed to help you navigate Earth. It oversees your efforts to keep your body and life going, but it is not *you*.

Pull yourself together before you decide upon the course you need to take to get to the end of this life. If you let it all hang loose now, most likely you will end up short of your goal. If you try to pack a lot of work into life, most likely you stretch your life span. If you sit and talk, doing very little while others do a lot, you may be given credit for helping them, but still lose if you did not complete your work.

Begin each day with a prayer of thanksgiving and you will know peace. Begin the day with war or games of divisiveness and you will be in turmoil that day. You cannot be at loose ends and tighten your life! Begin to realize you control all the ends and pieces, and *you* are responsible for the life you live here on Earth.

If you do not have any need to be here—you have no work you must do now, but you might be here to help others. This is not often the case, but it does happen. If you were so overloaded with burdens in a prior life that you did not have time to enjoy it, you may decide to return in order to fully understand why you had so much work then, or you may return to see what others did with your work of the past, or you may be intrigued by the entire idea of dedicating a lifetime to helping others. Whatever, you came here to do something!

If you do nothing—and you have that choice, you will return, if only to do what you came to do this time, plus a few other chores tacked on. So be sure you do all you came here to do this time. If you sit and look at others doing their work, you may feel guilty and try to stop them from working, but that never works. You still have to do your work. They will advance further than you, because they work while you idle.

What if you sat still and did nothing for seven days and seven nights? You could not. You cannot sit still and do nothing at all! The body left alone works. The mind is always busy, and Spirit soars when the body is not physically active. So how can you say you are doing nothing now? You have to do something while here, so why not do your work?

The world is never as hard on you as you are on yourself. You may think others are critical, which makes you angry, but nobody criticizes you more than you do. The ego is constantly demanding and nagging you to do certain things to improve your financial standing. The body will announce loudly it needs something, and Spirit is always waiting for you to do your work here. It is you who have to tune into *The Holy Spirit!* It does not demand, nag, or announce its presence.

Some brag they never rest, dream, meditate, pray, or even sleep long. Why? They are letting everyone know they are not all right. If you do not do all you can to prolong your life, obviously it will end sooner, rather than later. If you smoke, drink, and eat a lot of food, you may become obese, asthmatic, and alcoholic, yet survive; but what kind of life do you have? You need to determine if you want a shorter, longer, stronger, less lovely, more beautiful life, or whatever now—then do whatever it takes to accomplish it.

Some people go so far as to wish themselves dead. Why? Usually it is done merely for effect. They merely want others to pay attention to them. They do not feel noticed enough, or they are demanding others pay them what they believe is owed them, but such a ploy seldom, if ever, works. Why? The body hears such a demand and immediately goes into action to create a scenario that meets your demands. If you ever wished you were dead, sickness is the final outcome—or perhaps an accident.

You decide daily what your mood will be. Why be so negative? You are a positive being of light, and energy is not induced by crossing it with negative thinking. In fact, choosing to be negative may shorten your life—short you out, so to speak.

The time to begin seeing yourself as you are is right now. Do not delay a day! If you are in the worst possible mindset you can have, or flying without wings in a state of high mania, you cannot see yourself clearly. You need your feet fully planted on Earth with your head in the clouds, but to remain level your feet must not be higher than your head. You cannot let emotions raise and lower instantly or in long bursts as it will create havoc in your central nervous system. Instead, you need to relax, rest, and enjoy life's burdens and honors with the same emotional state—calmness.

If you were unable to enter the world as you are, you would not be here. You create the world and then live in it. If it no longer suits your needs, change it and adapt a new role. You will not be able to understand all of this until you are ready to become a new person, but you can assume it is correct and begin ridding yourself of the old ways today.

Work now—you can rest later!

The work of today is much more important than any other work you did before, but some keep doing it wrong. Why not sit down and figure out how to do a lot of work and get it all done? Because you are unwilling to stop and start while working, but expect others to do it. What you need to do is always treat yourself as you treat others, in order to know who you are.

When we work on Earth we do not teach the way you do or even as we normally teach. We blend what we know into what you know to help *you* assimilate the easiest ways for you to comprehend difficult concepts. If you cannot understand this, you can never advance. If you advance without doing all your work, you will fail later when it is a serious problem to do so.

What you do to you while here on Earth is not the worst of all fates, but if you learn negative habits here, you may use them in higher realms, too. The outcome would harm You (the Higher Self), which is why we will not let you dabble in such practices without being chastised. What practices here are unacceptable to God—or to those above this plane? You will know when you cross over, but some ask for guidance now to learn if you are on the wrong path. Unfortunately, some of you are on the wrong path!

Do not ever again ask for insight into another's life. You cannot get such data without the help and permission of that person. Also, do not ask for help in contacting the deceased who once lived on Earth. If they wish to speak—fine, but if they are busy and you interrupt them, you can harm their energy systems.

Let your time here be better spent finding out who *you* are, rather than seeking others still near this plane to talk to about your life now. Some people charge large sums of money to talk to the deceased and do not. If they do, why should you pay them? You can speak to anyone in your family now departed while still on the next plane, but do not ask them to talk to you. It is enough that they can see and hear you!

Your efforts to enter the next plane while on this one are unacceptable to us or anyone else above you. End such futile attempts. Instead, act like you enjoy being here, then you can live well and have all you want or need.

Swift work is often done by those who cannot understand the work of others, but such work is seldom worth much. You need to excel at a few things before you can do it all. If your work speaks of love and attention, all want it. If you do shoddy work, no one cares about it or you. Be sure the price you ask for your labor and art reflects *you*—not the marketplace. If you cannot afford to sell it, do not. However, if you care to share your work, sell it at a price others can afford and you will enjoy profits from it.

If you cannot talk or see others now, you cannot know if your work is acceptable or not. You need never worry about that if you live in a large family. Living there prepares you for life better than any other arena, but it can also harm you.

Harm received in the arenas of life is not as bad as when you do not care for yourself and deliberately harm others. You cannot ignore a back condition in order to gain money, nor act as if your back is hurt to make more money. Either way you will pay for it in pain and sorrow, and get little to make up for living with a bad back ever after.

Sing up a storm of protest and you bring frowns upon the faces of some by calling to mind all they fear. When you sing, someone hears you even when you see no one else around you. The Higher Self or You of YOU may not understand your words, but the seldom-known YOU is best met via the words you speak and sing today. Be sure to sing loudly!

There may be six or seven times in any year when you feel down and glum for no good reason you know of then. Times when you are not as you normally are may represent deaths of *you* in *'previous worlds'*— grief you may still feel surrounding such lives. What you need to do then is sit and try to meditate to remove at least your present fears of death.

Only when ready...

Sit and stretch your feet out in front of you. Then let your head sag. Feel your body folding into itself until you are totally relaxed. This is the pose of defeat. It is the most complete way to relax your body and mind. When you completely relax in this manner, work is not to be done. You need such time alone. We can feel you straining to relax now.

Never be upset! You have us—and we are all great. Why not let everything on Earth go? Because you cannot! Be *you* and enjoy our time together here and now so you will be ready in the future for all you need to do then.

Chapter Fifteen

The outside world is not the only one in which you live, as you well know. Your mind is a world of its own and unknown to all others but you, and you know nothing of the worlds within those who live around you, even though you know them well here and now. Why do you think this is true?

You cannot know all there is about anything or anyone while still on Earth. You are here to work with limited resources and acquire what you need to succeed. If you cannot succeed, it is because you do not work. To work hard implies success, but is not necessarily so. Why? Some do not work intelligently.

Intelligence is the major difference between humans. You may have a lot of knowledge and encounter few obstacles, yet not succeed, but you are happy. You may have little knowledge, great obstacles, and succeed beyond all others you know now. You may succeed and never know happiness. All depends upon the proper allocation of what you know to your goal—not the goal itself.

This is the only time to know you. You have to learn much, including how to be you all the time. Some learn early, and some never do, but all leave Earth having learned something—even if here for only a day. You do not need a lot of time if you have the necessary resources. If resources are limited, you need a lot of time. Due to the difference in these two factors, you need to learn how to do many different things.

You may not think much, but do a lot, or you may prefer to think and do very little. It is your choice, but you do one or the other, which is why you may or may not succeed. You need to balance them if you want success.

The world-class liar is the one who says, *"I am me,"* when he knows not that he will never be able to know himself while here. It takes a very wise person to know the way of his or her life, yet it happens. You need to study psychology and apply that knowledge to *your* daily life. If you apply it to others' lives instead, you learn little if anything about your mind.

The world is full of people who study subjects they never apply to their lives. Why? The work of applying information is not what they wish to do. They prefer to keep away from hard work, as they believe it to be. You cannot avoid work and continue to grow or hope to reap the rewards of study. You have to work at it!

The world is not tomorrow...it is Today!

If you do your work, you learn much. To sit and study all day in a room filled with students is not necessarily the beginning of a long, rewarding career. You may never use all you learn, but you need such time to recognize you must work. It is the work you do while in school that determines your success, not the subjects you study!

Some of the time spent in school is wasted, but it must be. If you are to recognize the times of your life, you must first learn the difference between living and being. Your life is full of life only if you experience and sense you are alive. If you rush about daily, never really seeing anything or anyone, you learn to fear others and accept what is here. If you frequently turn inward and examine the material you have absorbed, you will see it is more of the same—not a real problem. Be sure to stop frequently or become overwhelmed one day with all you need to catch up on and do.

Whatever you do, do not call it work. If while working on a project someone asks you what it is, say you are designing a new way to do something you wanted to do, but never had the time to analyze before now. This prods the other person to respect you and the time spent on the project. More importantly, it identifies for us the reason you are wasting time on it. You see, *we think your idle time is our time to work with you spiritually*—any other time is idling, not work.

Where you work or what you do is not always your choice, according to what you say. We cannot agree. You never work anywhere you do not want to work. You would manage to get fired, retired, or back-out before being hired. You may only sit and stare at a wall, but you are doing something to remain there.

Whenever you idle, you feel it is worthless, yet it may be the most productive time of this life. Why? It is during such times you finally come to know why, who, and what you are. Once you decide to learn all you can about *you*, your life's work moves forward. Before this happens, you simply sit and wait idly.

What if you were to begin a new job and discovered the boss does not want you? It happens. If you ever find yourself in this position, you may not wish to leave or may try to leave but cannot. Why? It is designated as your problem now. You have to work your way out of it. If you succeed, you get more money and prestige. If you do not succeed, you lose the job. We suggest life is often filled with such problems, because *you* placed them there.

Why would *you* place obstacles in front of you now? We know you do it all the time. You want life to be more adventurous, wild, or whatever, but you do it—not us or your Guides. If you do it, figure out why. If you do not figure it out now, you will continue blocking yourself.

Wonderful worlds await you on the next plane, and the ones above it, but you have to leave this one to see what is above this world. Why stay here? You are afraid to leave. To fear anyone or anything is the biggest mistake you can make in life. You have to leave Earth and rise beyond it, so make your time here as easy as possible for *you*.

Do Not Fear—Live Now!

If you are unafraid of death, what else is there to fear? Nothing! All fear remains rooted in a basic belief that life ends at death—and it does not. You proclaim in all your belief systems that life is eternal, yet claim you cannot believe in reincarnation? How is this possible? You believe in one or none, because they are the same.

The only other way you can waste a life is to always be so upset you never enjoy it. Why would anyone wish to be constantly upset? It is a complex issue, not easily described, let alone defined, but it can be explained. Each person needs to sit alone and describe why they want to be miserable and why they deserve to be out of sorts during this life. Once you can do this, you know the end is not of any real concern and your life can begin now.

If your life ends before you said goodbye to all you loved, you may wish to return over-and-over-again to see if they remember you. This happens, but it is unwise to do it. Your life on Earth is over when you leave and should be allowed to fall into your *past*. If you cannot do that, you will be allowed to return one time to clear the air. That one time is enough, but some still want to return more often and cannot, so they may send you messages here.

Messages received from those beyond this plane are sometimes fake, but not necessarily. Many of those beyond this time and place can return to the plane above this one and speak directly through to you on this plane with the help of a channel or psychically-developed adept. If you wish to learn to do this, you can, but why bother? Your life is full of messages from others here that you neither respect nor return. You do not need messages from beyond to take you out of this world. First, you need to live here and do your work. Once you leave Earth, try not to return!

If you do your work, you do not have to learn it again; but once you learn how to do something well, it is difficult to let up doing it. You choose to return to such work again and again because you are familiar with it, which is why some return to live on Earth over-and-over again. Let it drop once you leave. Let it go and grow elsewhere. Expect advancement!

While on Earth you may not believe you know much about the work *you* does, and why you have to do it, but do it anyway. Your spiritual work becomes easier as time goes by, because you learn to love whatever you do a lot. If you love your work, it shows. Disagreeable work is never done quite as well, even if it passes others' inspection.

If work is not done well, why do it? Because you need to develop pride of self—not be awarded it. If you ever receive an award from your fellow man, be sure to accept it. Do not act like you are above such awards, because you are not. The accolades of Earth are seldom given, but if they are, they should be accepted graciously.

You will learn that awards in this life are not of worth, but they help others honor your work and perhaps enter into it, too. If you do not realize this, you may be proud and believe they are recognizing you, rather than your work. If you let this happen, you will not be popular.

Working in the old *World of Yesterday* is not a wise idea, but you may decide to develop a living doing restoration work. You then have to watch that you do not lose your present life while working on the past. The past helps you gain perspective, but robs you of your time here. Be open to the present so tomorrow can welcome you. If you do not open to it, you will stall and become unable to move forward.

What if your life completely stalled out? You would be stuck in one area your entire life. You would never move or grow. You would sit out this life on your front porch and never enter the world. You would become grumpy, crabby, and unfriendly. Before you decide to reject it, be sure you can take this world's rejection.

The only other people you can hope to know well are those not present around you all day. If you work side-by-side with someone, you learn to not bother them. You learn to ignore their idiosyncrasies and respect few things about them, otherwise, you forget they exist. If you see someone only a few times a day, you learn to love their differences and respect them for who they are. We know this is why you choose to live and work in separate worlds today.

Children are not of either world. You may live with a child at home and notice the child is there and not there most of the time. A child has to learn to adapt to this atmosphere, and learn to live as humans live now—most likely having lived in other times and places. You can see a child leave its mind and body to enter another place, but cannot follow. Childhood is the time to let children learn who they are. If you prevent children from following their paths, you obstruct their view of life and prevent them from knowing who they truly are.

The older you get, the harder it is to learn. You fear you may not be learning anything, but you are. You cannot live and not learn. You cannot be here on Earth and not see the difference it makes when you are all you can be and doing all you came here to do.

If you think you are dead, get moving quickly, because you could end up dead. The body is not a computer. It does not shut down and end its day if there is no more data to compute. It continues to compute and digest its food and work building energy. If you do not use that work, the body will overload and die.

What if you ate so much that your stomach ached and you felt awful? You do it all the time, so why ask about it now? You constantly ask such stupid questions. Why? You do not listen to the answers. You know, but ask anyway. Why? You want to be reassured there is someone out there listening to you now. Why? You are not sure if you are alone here. Why? You vaguely remember someone else was with you when you came to Earth.

The only time you are unaccompanied by your Spiritual Guides is when you dwell solely within your ego. If you live within the confines of your mind and never meditate, you will discover your Guides are not there. They cannot enter the mind. They are forbidden to take over your life or devote all their time to you. If you call, they answer. If you never call or ask for help, they are free to be. *Free* is not exactly what is meant, but it answers the next question. Why would you let anyone else into your life?

Freedom of the mind is different from the usual definition of freedom. It implies you have the means to be yourself at all times, but may not seek it. You are confined to your mind if you stay within it at all times. You cannot comprehend the freedom of living this life if you dwell only within your mind.

This life is one of freedom versus lack of it. Freedom also exists on different planes and at different times, even as you live on this plane and exist in this world. What if you were to lose your way and enter another plane and not find your path? You do it all the time. You often forget the overall reason why you came to Earth!

You will accept *anything* at times, rather than do your work. Why? You are lazy. Something happens to the mind if it is not properly educated or stimulated. If it is not properly prepared for life, it becomes hard, brittle, and lazy. It breaks down and needs constant attention. It is not well-organized and may even go *'crazy'*, but it is not the purpose of this book to go into such nuances of disorganization. Why you came to Earth is not related to why you misarrange this life once here.

What you need to do to get onto your life path is not difficult to find out, but to do the actual work is thought to be difficult by most people. Why do it then? It is your life!

If you do not do your work here and now, you come back again and have twice as much to do then. If you do it all now, *you* can be free. There is no word that better expresses life than *freedom*, but it does not begin to explain why you feel free whenever you are being you.

You must let life go! If it is to be, it will fly and soar. If it is not, you will crash to Earth. Why not be sure you have the right flight plan before taking off? It will help you fly.

The only work of this world not of this world is what you do during meditation. If you sit and labor, so to speak, you cannot take any of it with you when you cross over. If you labor while meditating, you learn skills that are transferable and that dreams come to be.

There are seven ways to enjoy life:

1. **Eat**
2. **Sleep and eat**
3. **Sleep, eat, and sing**
4. **Sleep, eat, drink, and sing**
5. **Sleep, eat, drink, sing, and dance**

6. **Sleep, eat, drink, sing, dance, and love**
7. **Live and do all you wish.**

The only way to live and become all *you* wish to be is to try it all! How can you do it all in one life? You cannot. You have to come back again and again to do it all. However, most people have already done it all! So why bother trying to do it all again now?

Listen to the heartbeat of another and you hear a heart beating, but listen to your own and you realize you are alive. Why would you want to listen to others tell of their lives if you can do it, too? If you cannot live, listening is second best—but always second best.

The Scribe is not one to talk about her adventures, but she has many. Why would she not tell you about them in these *Books of Wisdom*? She is not writing them. She is channeling all this material, and it takes only a few hours of dedicated work on her part to do the entire work of art we have spent eons creating.

You do not have to live out the entire life of another to learn from them. Simply condense your lives in the past into one life and live it fully—then move on. You do not have to return again!

This chapter has progressed back to its beginning, we want you to do the same thing. How? Sit and stare at this page and imagine you are no longer here.

Now sit and stare at one word before you go any further with this work:

FREE?

Why are you not free?
What does freedom do for you?
What will you do now?
Why not be free?

YOU ARE FREE!

Chapter Sixteen

The only opening to the future you need is the one you are headed toward now. If you open one door in front of another they may or may not help you; but if you open doors as you grow, you will be able to advance in a straight line and shorten the trip to the top.

Debts and other forms of liability in this world are formed by you, but 'karmic' debts are from the past and recur or occur whenever you can handle them. So if you feel everything is going great and all of a sudden—WHAM, you opened a door and are ready to clear out what accumulated in this life or before. It is truly a great day!

If you never get to the point where you can clean out your house, it will become cluttered—maybe filthy. You have to clean out your life, too. You cannot sit out your entire life, never acting upon what you must do while here. If you could, you would be done—and out of here, so you could come back again to do what you have to do. Do you understand?

When you came to Earth you may have decided to clean up old, outstanding debts to the rest of the universe and also tackle a few other matters while here that may or may not affect others you knew in the past. If you think back over this life a distance and see some people are no longer a part of it, you recognize you met them, did what you came to do with them, and then moved on. It is that simple!

To dream of the day when you do nothing is to dream of death. You cannot sit still. You cannot enjoy idleness. You have to move. If you sit still and let all your energies flow into the ground, the Earth is enriched, but you are depleted. If you take all of the energy Earth provides in order to enrich you and others, Earth is depleted. You have to balance that energy.

How would you begin to give back to Earth the energies you have used or abused? You can begin by planting many different species of flowers for the bees and butterflies, never spraying insecticides on them. Learn to use mosquito repellant when you need it and otherwise let mosquitoes grow and thrive as before so fish can live. You can also eat less!

How do you think others feel when you appear to be fat and overfed? Do you represent everyone in your world? Not at all! You are unable to do that. You must know food is not in such abundance that some can eat all day while others barely eke out a single meal. This imbalance is occurring now and will get worse as more and more learn to abuse the efforts of others rather than share what they have here.

As you learn to use Earth to your advantage, the only way you can help others without raising your *'karmic'* debt level is to enjoy life one day after another—not store goods for future famines you plan today. Yes, famines are planned by those who have stored much. They can thrive and indulge themselves when others starve in order to assert they have more money or power than the rest of humanity. It is a very foolish game played only by fools, but still played today. You can see some amassing storehouses now full of grain and whatever they believe will be in short supply. They will be left with all of it!

The world will end for all—not just a few, If that is God's will!

The only one now not upset by the world's preoccupation with supply and demand is the one pulling all the strings. Who is that? God is not pulling this world's strings. God is not of this world. You are of this world and create it every day in every way, but God is not in it. You are the creation of God—and so is Earth, but not this world.

You are totally responsible for this world and its leaders! If you have leaders, you must be willing to follow them. If these leaders are useless, it is your fault. What if you saw the name of a totally degenerate human being on the ballot, would you vote for that candidate? Yes, many of you do that now. Why? You obviously believe such people will help you. If it helps you personally, you do not care about what is good for the average person or even the entire society. You need to decide now to end this regime of powerful people who are not interested enough in this world to do their jobs properly.

When offering others higher authority, you need to check and see if they can accept or not the larger responsibilities that go with the job. If they can, fine. If they cannot, elect another and another until you find a body of people who can properly govern all—not sworn to do the will of only a few. It may take ten elections to get the best people working together, but it will be better to do it that way. Let those who govern with wisdom remain in power, rather than every few years reelect the same bad apples from a barrel too deep to easily see the bottom now.

You never know if the people you elect work for all or not? Of course, you do! You watch television every day. Do you see nothing weird or strange going on in your capitals now? It is obvious. You cannot miss it! Do you immediately throw them out? No, you wait until everyone forgets their wrong-doings, then again place their names on the ballot and even re-elect them. That is stupid! Name names and strike all from your ballots for all time if they do something mean-spirited or evil. They should not be given another chance to break the public trust.

If you continue to elect poor officials and reelect the worst of your society to do what needs to be done for all, you will be unable to finish your lives here on Earth. The evil of doing business with the enemy is by far the worst sort of *patriot*, yet they exist everywhere in your world now. Why arm your enemies? You believe in your superiority only— and all will suffer for such egotism.

God is within everyone—even your enemies. Be sure you are of God or your enemies could strengthen the God-force within them and one day soon control you. Germany has prepared mentally for another outburst of war, but Americans do not notice much. You are all prepared, you think, for whatever comes. You are all fools! One loves to war and the other loves to believe it is invincible. What a war it will make! Japan is neither loose nor tight, but extremely overcrowded. Why or when do you think it will expand? It has to expand or die. You must not be afraid of a country that needs room, merely give it space—or lose it later.

The only world-class lecturer you will recognize will appear on television. Regardless of where that individual resides, she or he can address millions in a moment of time via that medium. If a dictator like Hitler were to rise again, the whole world would be there waiting to follow him. Scary, is it not? You created the monster, you have to tame it—not God.

God is entering the work of television and will continue to use it if it serves the best purposes of all mankind, but not if it sets one group against another as it does now. You have devised a method you can use to correct perceived errors in others' viewpoints, but it is not working as planned. It has cost your societies millions and millions of dollars in lost lives and property to recognize children are the biggest consumers of filth and smutty material—not adults.

When will you assume the role of parents and not betray your children? It could be too late for more than half of your population now. If evil children are permitted to end their lives as they started them, you will be tortured to death as adults. You will be unable to escape their evil when they have the power—and you created it! Why? Greed!

You coveted material things costing more than you could easily pay and were unwilling to work for your family as previous generations did. Without interest, you left your children to raise themselves. Such evil as is done to them will be repaid with interest in the future. You need not steer—rather encourage them to find God. If each child connects to God, the godly will overcome evil ones. However, if you do not know God, how can you teach others?

When you sense the need for the evil within you to erupt, do you let it happen? Some anger is just that, and some sex is nothing more, but neither is evil in itself. You are what makes either evil or good.

When the end comes, you will be the only ones not wanted on Earth. All other creatures will be able to survive, even animals and insects, but you all will be banished! The only tangible thing you all can do now is end the strife among nations. If the world ends now, all are in harmony or not, but it is not as bad as it could be. If you work to harmonize the entire planet and balance what is wrong with what is good, you all could continue here for millions of years. It is a human decision—not God's—to end life as you know it now.

If God knew *you* before you arrived—and let you come to Earth, why would God not let you stay? If you chose to do what you know is evil, and appear to do no good, it will end all existence for *you*. If a human being is so evil he or she cannot remain on Earth, murder of the soul takes place here or afterwards, but it does take place.

If you have already had two opportunities to save your life here, you do not get another chance. Never believe God is all patience and understanding. That is heresy. You do not know God and never will, so do not put words into the mouth of God.

Many past ages have arrived upon Earth and still linger waiting to be investigated at your leisure, once you learn how to do it. You cannot learn from the past if you are stuck in evil here. You would only learn more evil, so you cannot go back. If you demonstrate your ability to do only good for others, as well as yourself, you may be given more and more advantages you earned in other times—or maybe not.

What you need on Earth now is discipline!

You hear about discipline all the time, and many laugh at the idea. You shirk responsibility every day for disciplining evil-doers. You pay people to remove them from the public domain, then free them. What a game! You all will be losers in the end. When you free an evil person to do more evil, you do it with the intention of helping them. However, if one is educated and can do evil legally, you cry that money is wasted educating criminals.

You are all so confused! If you continue to be confused, you may never know who you are. Why not sit down before you have no time left and decide who is to be killed for what they did against mankind, who is to be imprisoned, and who is to be shod and fed at public expense. These three decisions will solve millions of your world's problems. What you do now is not always wise, but has to be done, or so you say—so do it! If it turns out poorly, erase it, and do it over again.

Why are you not doing something about evil-doers now? You are afraid of what will happen to you one day, if you continue what you are doing now. That can be the only reason you do not respond with outrage today.

What if you see something evil is not encouraged nor discouraged by others, would you decide to do it, knowing you would be caught? No! You do much that is evil now in order to escape punishment of the ordinary sort—such as lessons in thrift or work.

You do not want to save resources or work hard, rather end your days trying to steal the work of another. Such theft is acceptable in most businesses now. When a worker is found to be totally inept, do you ask for his resignation or fire him? If he is not obnoxious or a threat—probably neither. If you fear he may not be able to control obvious misbehavior, you may get rid of him—or not. If you personally fear him in any way, you will definitely fire him, thus trying to send a message to others not to try it, too.

The work world is strictly man-made. Women are trying to enter the game and assume roles of dominance, and some men will let them, but most men will get another game going instead. That is okay! Why? They do not have anything else to do here.

The work of the world is a pastime until you move up to the next plane. Few are here for long or willing to spend all their time here, so there is no time to waste on games; but it is the way of men to have at least one game going at all times. Remember, games are not real life— only a means of forgetting you have one.

What you do with your life while on Earth is of great concern to some people—usually women. Why? Women are more fully aware of the role of creation and dedication of their lives to service, as well as the need to work diligently every day. Men are less mature in some aspects, and almost always more ego-driven, but if a man is driven to do good or evil, no woman has the dedication such a man gives to complete the task.

What if you decide to end your life? Do you often say such things? You are not the only one who is not welcome at times on Earth. All suffer fears of rejection and abandonment, but most control them. If you do not, you will earn no one's respect, and your remains are usually forgotten. You must never threaten God, either. If you do, *you* will end.

There are few of you developed enough to enjoy conversing with the universal God of All, but if you ever are, enjoy the expansion of your soul. Do not boast of it or risk being criticized as not being sane by both God and man.

We are not teachers of your plane, but we can teach on your plane. Do you wonder how that can be? You have only to ask us. You can be told much about what is, but you should not question who is. The work of others is not that difficult, but you cannot do it.

You have not evolved—and you may or may not evolve! It is your work at each stage that determines if your soul gains or loses. If you gain, you evolve beyond this plane or whatever plane you are on then. If you lose, you are no longer *you*.

Whatever you do while on Earth to deserve poor treatment is generally what lingers later and evolves into your next assignment. If you do nothing here of use to *you*, why think you would be advanced? You must use your native intelligence to advance and gain spiritually while here.

Not thinking for yourself ends poorly!

There are many within the realm of angels. There are not as many within the realm of man, and this realm is not as large. You seem surprised, why? Because you are not that great? Nonsense! Angels are not any different from us or you. We are all of God. All of us work. All of us aspire to raise the vibrational level of the universe. We are all here to learn.

Yes, angels are here on Earth, too! The old age of angelic realms is still here, but the new one is quite different. From old artwork you learned angels often came to Earth in olden days—visiting in robes, wings, and haloed heads, surrounded by cherubim, seraphim, and cherubs floating all about. They did appear!

Today angels are not appearing as they did in the past, instead they are felt. If you can see an angel, you are greatly relieved, but know they are around you even now. People here do not realize angels are not their servants or helpers, but are sure angels care about them. Why? Why would another of God's creations care about you? Perhaps you were assigned to one of them—ever think about that?

Assigning Spiritual Guides, angels, and others to you while here may sound like a fairy tale, nevertheless, it is true. You may be so overloaded with work from higher realms that you need help doing it now. If so, your household is filled with helpers of another realm. All you do is not always what you want to do. You feel you must paint, paper, and fix up, even though it may not be what you set out to do?

Angels are enemies of dirt. They despise it! They are not comfortable anywhere there is darkness or dirt. You will notice if you clean your home that it is less likely to be invaded by an enemy. You will learn that bugs are not enemies, but can be pests. People, however, can be both enemies and pests. If you fix all you inhabit to the highest level you can, your enemies seldom enter your area.

Why would a home be a source of an enemy's failure? You are most likely to be *you* when residing within the walls of your abode. If you project any energy at all, it is magnified when surrounded by your things. You have selected certain elements of pleasure to surround you there, and you keep certain things. Why? They have intrinsic meaning to *you*. You may not know why they are there, but you keep them anyway.

There is no one on Earth who does not have at least one object they cherish. You will leave Earth before you realize why. It is not that you all are collectors or trash-keepers. You merely think of the day you got that particular item and remember it. If you have a house loaded with such things, you live entirely too much in the past. If you leave such things behind every time you move, you lose yourself. Balance is required. What if you never move, thus it just accumulates? Rid yourself of it all, so you can decide where you are going now and why.

Work is never the place to be if you want to play, but many play at work. Why? They know no other people! You need friends. You need to be able to laugh! If you are to grow, you need to go places and do things other than your normal work routine.

When you mix anything, you cause it to become confused. If you confused a machine it would break down. If you mix pleasure with business, you gain less of each. You will not enjoy what is done in one vein when another is intended.

We work in one area—you in another. We cannot intermingle! You cannot intermingle at work, either. If you mix business and pleasure, neither occurs—or it is so mixed that no one knows what happens. The government has induced some people to mix business and pleasure in order to tax such occasions, but a business that insists you do business when you are socializing is wrong, too. Most business luncheons are not about eating, so why do it?

You cannot eat, talk, and conduct business at the same time. Instead, you induce much stress. When stressed, sit in the dark and ask for realization of what your life is now. Once you see yourself as you are, you are *you*. We believe most of you can do this by merely closing your eyes. For some it is not all you need do to block extrasensory perceptions (ESP).

ESP is not the way to refer to extrasensory perception, but it surely is not the worst thing to describe people who are *'gifted'*. You may not be gifted, but understand others are; yet you cannot give them credit, because most humans are too tough at center. They demand others to be like them. This is impossible, but still many make such demands.

You can be extra-anything. You do not have to be gifted to have more than another, but it helps. When you desire something others take for granted, you can help yourself by taking lessons from them or condemn those who have it. How do you approach life today?

It is the habits of a lifetime that denote the character of a person—not how they were raised. If your family chose you to do something continually, you may believe you alone possess that capability in your family—may even believe it extends to all the world, which is self-delusion. You can do whatever you wish, and can try a lot of other things as well, but if gifted with whatever, you worked hard to achieve it in another life episode and can do it now without apparent difficulty or study.

Work to become all you ever wanted to be and sometimes the gift arrives belatedly, but it arrives! When it does, be assured it is not to be wasted. A gift is not to be ignored long or it disappears. Your life is not a gift, but many abilities and talents which give you an easier life are. If you want to be gifted with more, be sure to appreciate what you already have!

This is the end of a long, arduous trek into the mind of everyone reading this book. If you fear anyone here, lead them back to the beginning. Start reading each sentence backwards—sentence-by-sentence. It will drive you, or those you fear, crazy long before you get to the first sentence of this chapter. If it does not, read the entire book backwards.

Confusion is not the least of the mind's ways of cleansing you of Spirit's influence. However, more than any other method, it results in many being misled. Be sure you remain clear-headed, sharp-witted, and keen-sighted when you peer into the inner realms of your life—because there you will see *you!*

Second sight is not the use of your eyes, rather the outcome of seeing life. Be sure you enjoy yourself and live now—all is grand then! Be of little use to others, enjoying nothing, you may as well have left Earth, but you would have to come back and do it all over again.

This is the end of a long litany of confusing thoughts and ideas for some—and the beginning of insight for others. Decide now, then acknowledge which describes you best. We will wait for you to catch up before beginning the next chapter. Be ready!

Chapter Seventeen

The only work you need to do in order to see the future is: Look at you today! The only work you will do is what you choose to do, thus the future is entirely based on your decisions and your work now. No one can deny what you wish for or take credit for it. You have all you need to accomplish whatever you wish to do, but also have the ability to stop all you wish to do, too.

Why would you stop yourself? We often ask *you* that. You are so full of *self,* and at times jealous enough of others to stop doing something in order to prevent them from sharing in your wealth or progress. You are greedy enough to stop living well in order to accumulate as much as possible, rather than risk losing a bit to reach your goals. You are also evil enough to want only you to succeed.

Alone, these behaviors can harm you, but the harm you permit others to do to you is the biggest crack in your armor. You often let others do unto you what you would never do to them. Why? Some actually believe their religion condones such practices, but none do. Some believe others know or deserve more than they do, but they do not. Some believe you are not all you can be now, and need less-and-less as you grow in wisdom—they are right!

What you do is not who you are? Wrong! You are—and you do. You cannot be anyone if you never work. You must grow into roles of this life. If you assume you do not have to work, you lose that role to someone else. If you do not like a role, you may lose on purpose. We care not why you lose roles, only if you wanted to lose or not. If you have no further use of a role, fine. If you lost it due to lack of interest in doing enough work to maintain it, *you* lose.

Do not let others determine who you are or why you are here. If you do not, they will. Do you let others help you, then not aid them in return? That is wrong, and all are aware of it, but few know why it is wrong.

You do not have to work for others—unless you ask them to work for you. If you ask others to work for you, make them aware of all you are or they will not understand who they are working for and why. If you reveal enough about yourself to work well together, you did all the socializing you need to do then. If you socialize more than that, you risk imperiling all you have. Some become too intimate with a few of their workers and lose the respect of all. If you lose the respect of others, blame yourself!

The future of your life in the business world is never in jeopardy as long as you work hard and do not act like you are in charge. If you are in charge, you need to act like it is not your only interest in life or others will try to disband your organization in order to defraud you or get what you have. If you support such a person, you could lose when they are ousted, so be sure you, too, keep many irons in the fire. When you have only one job and one wife, you have fewer problems than when you have several of one or the other, or both.

It is the object of some men to amass great wealth in order to have more of everything, but they eventually discover they have nothing. Why? If your world is in conflict, you cannot handle as much work. Conflict is not the result of strife, but inner turmoil.

You must be able to determine who you are and why you are, before you end a relationship of long-standing. It is not as complicated with a short-term romance or fling, because such episodes usually end within days of discovery, so why bother with them? If your romances are of no worth, and you would throw them away if discovered, why continue wasting your time? Ego!

Ego is the means to all of man's self-contamination. You cannot ask others to be your slave, your love mate, your spouse, or friend, then do nothing for them in return. You are enslaved by love—obligated to befriend all of them. Too much is too much and can lead to trouble for all involved!

Work uses less energy and demands far less of you. If you work on what you enjoy doing rather than what pays best, you will be happier than those with a lot more money—and you will end up with a lot more of whatever you want now. Why? You do not have to go out and spend a lot to become happy if you already are. This critical difference is not noticed early in life, but becomes apparent as you age—and is much envied by others.

What you do today is not much different from yesterday or tomorrow, but over a long period of time you can see a trend. If your present trend is to be short-tempered and ill-natured, you will have few friends. If you have few friends, but continue to work on being friendly and helpful, you will end up with many friends gathered around you. It is similar to seeding a garden. You end up with what you plant—only you reap more than you thought you would at the start.

What you do now is not as important as what you will continue to do in the future. Never do something once and expect a reaction of long duration! Do you do that now? You may, but it is not realistic, because few actions are that drastic.

When you work on work you love, you spend fewer hours with others. Why? You are already happy and do not need to be entertained. If you are unhappy? You end up with a lot of time on your hands, and few hours are filled with good times, even if you are never alone. Be ready for times when you have no one around. Be happy regardless of whether or not you are alone.

Some people play games to pass the time of this life and become good at it—while others ignore such games. Why pass your life in idleness not shared by others? If you never do anything others can appreciate, you do little to improve your life. If your life is full of fun, you probably do not play games!

Sit down and search out all the things you do now that encourage others to approach you. Do you have a long list or a short one? Does it have a lot of crowd-pleasing events on it? Are you a loner? Do you prefer small events to large ones? Why? Do you know why you avoid crowds? Do you care about large groups now? Do you care if you are excluded from groups? Why? Once you can answer all of these questions, you know a lot more about yourself than when you started this paragraph.

How can one short sentence or paragraph change your life? It can if it gets you to think. If you think—you do! If you do, you change. If *you* change, so will your world. If your world changes, the universe changes, too. So think, and think, and think, until all you are is who you are, and you know who *you* are.

When the end of your work on Earth is done, after crossing-over you arrive on the other side without anything left from this Earthly experience but a few ideas. You will be asked to circumscribe these events and deliver a short memorandum of the events and cases you worked on while on Earth. Will you be stuck then or will you have many areas you can choose from? Decide now!

Work here is not like work on other planes, but the details are the same. If you do not pay attention to details now, you will. If you are a nit-picking critic of everyone and everything, you will be pecked to your dying day by others who are not as nice as we are. Yes, you can be pecked—look at you now! You do it to you all the time. If you all did less nagging and more work now, everyone would be happier.

What if you do not like your work? You can do it anyway, but it would never be as pleasing as what others do who enjoy their work. Some envy those who do work very well that they hate. Why envy someone who does work you hate? You may not understand why, but you do work well that others hate to do, too, so enjoy what you do well and let others enjoy what they do well.

If you all played fair,
Everyone would be happier!

What if your team this life is not good at what needs to be done now? What if you picked the wrong mate or had too many children? What if you never had a good job or cannot find one? What if you said nasty things to your mother and she left you alone for life? What if you were unable to enjoy anyone—including you? You are full of ego and expect others to do your work while here!

Ego and unmet expectations are your failure to recognize others also exist—and are not here to do your bidding. They, too, are here to work. If you cannot do your work, you still have to let others do their work or live to regret it. When you expect others to do what you do not want to do, or do not know how to do, you are less envious than if you know how to do it or could do it alone.

If another does a much better or poorer job than you would have done, you will be unhappy about it. It is impossible for two people to work exactly the same, so do not set yourself up for disappointment by thinking you can. How often you think like that depends upon how slow you learn this life's lessons.

Whether or not you learn fast or slow—you learn, even if it takes all this life. You came here to learn and you will! If you cannot learn due to definite disabilities, you will be shown leniency. Different degrees of ability merit different rewards. Some are disabled only for a short time and then miraculously cured, while others seek health every day of this life. Usually, this is due to the urge to be someone other than you. Yes, you do wish at times to be someone else and do things you were never intended to do while here on Earth—which leads to danger and accidents.

The only time you are involved in an accident is when you stop concentrating on who you are now. You like to think accidents are not created on purpose, but they are. They occur in order to make you concentrate on the here and now. If you continually account for your time in a certain way and then suddenly forget it, you are not concentrating and an accident is likely to happen. It was not that someone else was after you or cared if you were caught up in a fall or whatever. It is caused by your own inability or unwillingness to concentrate on what you are doing in the moment.

Work is not without mystery

Like putting together pieces of a puzzle, you have to do a certain amount of work on faith before it starts making sense, but if you do it long enough, you develop speed and accuracy, and may even become extremely competent. **Remember**: Initially you had to work without knowing for sure it would all fit together.

Wherever you are now is fine. The future will be less or more than it is now if you change your actions today. Be sure you change to gain rather than lose what you have. You always decide what you do this life!

After this hard-working chapter you deserve a long rest, so we end by asking you to do a few more things:

1. Put your life into the middle of this work and ask for help only if needed.
2. Pull yourself and your friends into the middle of all you are doing now and see if all are compatible. If some are not, you would be wise to prune away what is incompatible with your work now or be sorry later.
3. Put your life in order now and keep it in line.
4. Expect no one else to do what you can do. This leads to self-satisfaction with few disappointments.
5. End all relationships that now linger. They will only hurt more and more as time goes on.
6. When many work at one job, pull your weight and you will always be welcomed by them.
7. Go into the night and seek what you fear. Darkness is not an enemy, but light can be if you live in the shadows.

We go now to return on another day. **Remember**: Study is not work! Study enhances the mind—not the body. The body is deliberate in its attempt to shirk what is not its work. You will know what we mean!

Chapter Eighteen

The World of Tomorrow is about to begin! Let your mind flow and let your heart grow. Know it! You are in the midst of The New Age now. You, too, will know it when you see it.

What if your life is never as deep or as beautiful as God intended it to be? Would it be your fault—or caused by someone or something else that failed *you*? Why not let your life be all it is and grow beyond your widest and wildest dream of life on Earth? Why not enjoy all of this world, all people, and all the animals, plants and organisms that produce your world? Can you do that?

When you let your mind wander and roam over the universe (we assume you do that at times), do you ever see strange things? If so, you are already inside the new *you* and able to enjoy The New Age. If you cannot remember ever seeing anything strange or weird, you inhibit yourself so as to never be afraid, thus hurting your chances of entering The New Age now.

Worthwhile beings live in this universe and are not human. You are human. You live on Earth—and you are not totally alone. You share this planet with many other beings and have the knowledge to use many of their greatest discoveries, but will you?

When the day comes for you to go out into the other side of this life, will you be ready? Not if you cannot meditate now. Why would you want to do anything new if you cannot find time to fully live on Earth now? You believe your life here is very complex, but why? If so, you are not working enough on your inner life.

What you learn daily while here on Earth is not of such great depth that you cannot learn much more, but you may think you have no time to study or feel too lazy to work harder than you are now. What do you want from life? Do you want to grow? Do you want to know all you can about this life? Are you afraid to find out that you are not so special?

The ego is afraid to be found out! The ego cannot understand its place is temporary. It believes it is in total control, and you let it believe that. You are guilty of betraying your mind at times. How? You let your ego believe it is in charge—and it is not.

The spiritual aspects of your personality rule you all the days of your life while on Earth and beyond. You are not here to begin anything new or even make a big discovery. You are here to learn to manipulate the Earth plane, then go onto another plane, and another plane, and another.

If you stay locked inside your mind, you can never grow. Yes, some can grow and some cannot, but it is your choice always which group you belong to or decide to live with now. Once you learn to adapt to the Earth plane, you may become so attached to it you cannot or will not let go when you die. Why not let it all go and enjoy the tributes and accolades given to you then for having traversed the Earth plane successfully? You do not know if you will get any? Then you are afraid of being judged unworthy.

If the final judgment of your lifetimes on Earth is not to your satisfaction, you can ask to return. So why not let your work here be judged when you die? You could stop this endless cycle of returning constantly to Earth to 'perfect' a life that cannot be perfected while here. When you can better understand that life goes on whether or not you live on Earth, you will be able to end this repetition. Until then, let us not become so involved with the work of this world that we cannot enjoy it—nor so dedicated to it that all cannot rise above it.

Work is not the same on every planet, plane, or even on every level of a plane, but it can be. You do not have to change your job to get ahead now. You can learn that lesson while here on Earth. If your job is not going anywhere, you may learn you are not going anywhere here on Earth and decide to get off. Fine! We want you to start realizing life is a mirror of your eternal being, but not the same.

You will never see what this world is doing until you can do what you want and go where you like without fear. If you fear the streets outside your home, you do not venture forth. If you fear the local metropolis, you never go to that city. If you never go out, you are isolated and unable to fulfill the reason you came to Earth, which is: *to learn to tolerate others and be of service to all.*

What you need to do is clean up the yard and back-porch of every home in your country. If every house had a nice, neat yard, everyone in that house would want to go outside and live there for a time. If it is ugly, no one wants to linger outside, but it can invite others who are not evil or good to linger and develop into evil-doers over time.

Why are you so afraid of others—particularly if they are not quite like you, and most especially if they are very different than you are? Do you believe others are less in the world or less likely to succeed than you? You have to learn all about them before you can leave Earth! If you never meet, it is your life that is less—not theirs.

The only person who is unafraid of the dark is the one who dwells in the light of God. All others are unsure of the reason for life or death, thus unable to understand why they are on Earth. If they spot anyone or anything strange or unusual, they run or panic. The panic of some lives is so intense now they cannot stop running even when they are safe within the walls of their homes.

How can you explain to a child that life has value, if you are afraid to go out into it? You are the reason the child is here. You owe the child comfort, help, and the understanding you received as a baby and growing child—not what is seen as adequate care today.

When you cannot do something, you may fear it. Why not learn how to do it and settle that matter for all time? You learn only what you need to know, so you never learn anything you do not need.

There is a town on Earth where all the inhabitants are wise to the ways of the world, and you need a visa to enter their city. Why would you restrict the world from entering a perfect universe? You fear! If you fear, you are worse off than the free, unafraid man or woman of uncertain character who walks the streets of a huge city.

What you need to do to get your fear in check is develop your *Self*. You see, *Self* is not the same as soul, but yet it is. If your *Self* is different, why are you still the only one here who is you?

We would never correct your Spiritual Guides, but they often let you assume you are the only one in this world like you—which is not true. You are a double or duplicate of another *you*, one who dwells within this plane, but on a different level. The level below this one is not the same as hell, but it is not the same as this one, either. It is the duplicate of Earth, but it is not on Earth.

The Earth you live on now is not the Earth you are from. If you are here for another life you once lived on Earth, it was not the same planet as this one. You are confused by this? Then you do not realize there are many 'Earths' in the universe, and some of them are still in *The Dark Ages, Roman times*, or in the evolutionary stages of animal development. You are still there, yet you are here! It is not the same thing, but it is. We will enter this realm at another date, so you can absorb this message now and can learn a little bit more before we go beyond the present and enter the future.

How can you enter the future?

You wonder! You worry! You evolve! But you cannot decide if you want to leave the present or not—that is why you never leave NOW! The work of your life here is NOW, and the time to do it is NOW, but you will be here in the future, too. Right? No, not exactly.

You will now leave and enter the future—then return to NOW. You may decide to go back into the past and reenter the present before you go on to the future. It is not impossible to enter the present, but it is difficult to enter the future. Why is that? The time you live here is quite out of sync with the time we set-up for *you* within your future.

Since we discussed the subject of Time in great detail (**Now is The Time**, Volume Four of *The Books of Wisdom*), we will say only this now: You have to live within the time you are in, and believe you are in that time, if you are to progress spiritually. If you start clinging to a former time, you delay your life, and default on the goals you previously established due to a lack of time to complete them.

If you jump into the future while still working in the present, your anxiety level becomes so extreme you may even die of fright. Really! This is not the time to die or live. It is your time to be all you can be!

Even if you live, die, and go on to the next plane, you are still here. Why would you remain here? You do not want to leave Earth! We are here now trying to release you from ending your life when the eruption of time is over on Earth, or the planet descends into abject poverty of air and water and forces death on most inhabitants of your plane.

The only time to fear leaving Earth is when you still have a lot to do here. If you know your work is done—or nearly so, you feel a deep sense of satisfaction and attempt to do what you can to help others, but it may not be like that for all. Some will never be sure about their performance here. They are ruled by anxiety all their days on Earth and cannot assume anything, but the wise can assume much. If you know your work is good, assume you will be able to advance.

There are several people in the world who are unable to decide where they are or who they are, but the rest of the world is sure about them. It is so obvious you may wonder why anyone would believe in those who do not believe in themselves, yet all believe them to be capable of ruling great dominions due to an accident of birth. Royalty is not a guarantee of wisdom—only wealth. You must begin to question why you are driven to help some advance beyond you here.

What if your life on Earth was so demented you could not determine if you were here or not? You would be determined by the medical world to be schizophrenic and acknowledged as being *'disintegrated'* by psychic societies, but both are wrong. You are living at two different levels within the same plane and cannot determine which is which. It could happen to anyone at any time!

When your life is over and done, you will be unable to decide if it is of worth or not. You are not far enough removed from it to judge, but your Spiritual Guides can determine long before then if you are off-track or not. Your Guides will constantly force you to evaluate yourself if you are not on track, but seldom bother you if you are on course.

Your Guides can rest if you are busy, but if you idle, they are overwhelmed with your work. Why? They will be held somewhat responsible for not getting you to attend to your spiritual business while here. Their vested interest in your business is what keeps them trying to get you back on line and being a success. Be sure you know your Spiritual Guides, thus have no problem knowing where you stand now.

There are several places on Earth where you cannot do anything but survive. They will not let you enjoy yourself there, kill yourself, or do anything not condoned by the authorities. You may think we talk of prisons, but we are referring to universities.

Higher education is not higher. It is not anything at all like that. It is a spot on Earth where the air is so rarified only a few can utter pronouncements worthy of being repeated—and only a few are allowed to repeat those few words. Why would you want to go there? Because you are told you must have one of their sheepskins in order to get a good job. Is that possible? Obviously, it is.

When you decide to enjoy life, you discover you need work, but you do not need a certificate of accomplishment to do good work and succeed in the world. The certificate is of no value if you cannot do anything with it—literally. It has to be framed to be used even as a decoration—and it generally impresses only its owner. No one else values it, but some envy you if they do not have one.

Education cannot be bought or sold like a piece of dry goods, but it is being bargained away now. You have to senselessly give up untold dollars to get a little bit of information the educators at such a school say is what life is all about. They add up the days, weeks, months, and years you worked on their assignments to decide if you have enough credit to graduate. Time then is of the essence—not the degree of knowledge.

Whether or not you believe in education, you can see it has its merits. It is required if you are to know how to spell, write up a bill of lading, and work the proper amount of time each day you are employed by others; otherwise, you do not need much education to do what you naturally do best.

Even lawyers and doctors are not educated—rather trained. No one today is shown how to believe in the law, or how to enter the bar, or how to run an office well. Everyone is taught how to pass the entrance exams; and if you are lucky, how to manage to win your cases—not how to judge if the case has merit or not.

Only those truly aware are gifted and do not need an education. They take on what is taught or demanded in order to be permitted to practice what they already know. Healers are all born to heal, but papers must be issued that permit them to practice their art—thus the reason for medical schools today.

The only one honored without any certificate is the scholar of great worth. There can be no certificate to indicate how much anyone *knows!* No intelligence test has yet been devised or will ever be devised that can meter the amount of knowledge anyone has. The only criteria used now are massive doses of miscellaneous, detailed quizzes and tests which mean nothing. Essays are not of any use in determining wealth or health, but may help you know who can write. The mathematical skills taught today are so archaic that you will be unable to recognize them once you leave Earth.

The work of the world is not for You, but is of *you*. If you do nothing, you have nothing. At the last moment on Earth you will not be judged on how nice you look or how well you talk, rather how much you did while here. If you do nothing now, how will you look then? What will you say at the end?

There are several different ways to advance spiritually, but the only one you know now is to work hard every day and do what is right. If you harm or hinder anyone due to a difference of flesh tones or traces of ideology, you will be the lost sheep who is never found. Yes, indeed, there are sheep never found—not all are recovered!

There are various means of recovering from setbacks in life. Few are so difficult you cannot recover if you try. You have to do it alone, but often another interferes with your thought processes in order to deliberately get you to reevaluate who you are now and why you are here. If you are so far off track that you cannot know there is one, you will need a lot of help and guidance from both sides of the veil.

What if your friends in spirit are not friends?

There are some who cling to you beyond this life who are not of this life, but wish to help you. If they pass a few written exams, they can be certified to be your Spiritual Guide (we jest), but few offer to guide others once they go beyond this plane. Why? They still have their lives to live. If someone dear to you on Earth dies and asks to be your Guide, he or she may be allowed to do so as long as you are here on Earth, but that is not the norm.

We asked earlier: *What if one of your friends in spirit is not a friend?* You will not be bothered by them! You may ask to talk or even call out to them, but they cannot come forward and bother you. The Guides who direct your spiritual path are not going to let anyone bother you if they can stop it. They are protectors and advocates, but you have the power to override all of their help and guidance—even destroy your life here.

When you decide to go into the next work of this world, you will see a few people wince because you are not maintaining the old ways, but most will watch for a time to see if you fall or stumble, then go about their business. The same is true for those on other planes who may be somewhat interested in your behavior here.

Whatever you do now, it is your life and you cannot expect others to take credit for it, but you may give it away. Why? You are foolish enough to believe others will honor you for being generous, caring, and compassionate, but it will never happen! All honor the fact you did what they did not want to do, but they do not honor you above themselves ever.

When you see your life 'slip over the yardarm', as they say, you will know you did all you came to do—or not, but you cannot change it then. So be sure you have it all together as soon as you know what it is you came to do. It makes life much easier!

There are several other items we need to review with you before this chapter is through, but you need to take time now to develop what you now know about life in the future. If you can follow us, we will lead you….

Wow! Did you feel anything just now? We just leapt ahead one second! Did you feel anything? No? We did! We can see you leap and bound ahead at times like antelope playing in tall grass, but you neither see nor feel it.

We will explain more about it Tomorrow, that is if you continue to read our words and seek wisdom here. We will not delay you, because it is your decision to continue working now or not. No one else can decide even that much for you, so be aware of how your next decision might encumber you in the future.

Chapter Nineteen

The only world you know is the one in which you live, and you live in only one world at a time. If you could slip back and forth into more than one world, you would be unable to keep them all straight, so you do only one life at a time now. The work of this world is not the work of any other world!

If you learn to manipulate the atmosphere here and operate well within its confines, you will learn to do a few other things, too, that will help you in *future* lives on other planes. If you never learn while here, how can you expect to move beyond this plane now? If you are to continually learn, the work of any other world is not the same, nor should it be. You need to transfer your energy from one type of life to another while living here to learn how to do it on other planes; nevertheless, it is totally different elsewhere.

There are a few ways you can develop while on Earth that enable you to advance to the next plane and live easily there. Few are even aware of the existence of the next plane—let alone living there. Thus we are reluctant to advance such information now—you have to ask for it.

What if your life cannot keep *you* in place here? Yes, your life could take such a big jump that *you* cannot stay here. For example: You might decide to enter a coma and live for months in such a difficult climate that much of your body is not needed and does not respond to this plane. If *you* return to this life, you will enjoy living here more, but you may prefer to go on to the next plane instead. Your life here was unable to keep *you* here. Do you understand that concept?

While we are on the subject of comas, we would prefer not to delve into why you do that or why *you* decide to end this life in such a way, but be aware a coma is much like hypnosis and is total awareness—not you living on this plane so much as *you* in another mind. You have several minds, you know. Yes, you do!

When you absent-mindedly say: *"I must be losing my mind."* You are recognizing the fact that you can. You can totally lose the thread of a conversation if distracted or unable to complete a thought, but it does not mean you are insane or unable to function normally. It means *you* have several lives going on simultaneously and cannot decide which one is more interesting to live at that given moment, so you dart back and forth between them—usually two, but there could be three or more.

What about the times when you are so still you feel your body is dead? If you feel that way, you are. You can see the body is not going to respond if you are not active. You must keep active in order to make the body respond when needed. If you let the mind go on and on in a droning fashion—never tell it to be alert or expect a response then.

Where your heart sits is not where you are. Your heart is not the center of your universe. YOU are the center of your universe. Your heart keeps you going and pumps oxygen and blood into the body, but it cannot do it without *you*. However, you can use the body even if it does not have a heart. That is true! Such pumps can be replaced or mocked up, but you cannot.

Whatever you do and wherever you go, you are *you*, but you may not be living. Some of the time spent within your dreams is not while sleeping on this plane, but working on another. How can you know the time has come for you to do a lot of work? You become very restless, tired, or lonesome—such emotions cause you to change. You cannot tolerate any of them for long, so you change—and usually do it rapidly.

Do not inhibit yourself!

Do not let up on examining the way you work or how you see yourself. However, do not criticize yourself so much that you do not do your work. A critic within the mind is such a severe handicap you may have to end its life. How? You simply refuse to listen!

Work and do not look at anything you do. Do it and turn it out for the world to see if they think it is okay or not. If you find it is good, you can continue to do it. If you find no one else willing to buy it, you probably did not do enough work or need help. That is when you should criticize your work—but not until then.

We watch some work as if inspired by their egos, and we hear you say it is *'divinely inspired'* when it is not. If your ego cannot differentiate between manic and spiritual influence, you often ascribe higher sources as the means of creating your work when you are not tuned into either. How will you know if your work is divinely inspired? You do not have to sell it or explain it. Others understand it immediately!

What you do now is not as important as what you will do in the future. If you are unable to do anything well now, you may decide to do nothing—which is *not* a safe course to follow. It will lead to death on this plane with nothing to recommend you for advancement to the next one.

Be sure you work today so there is a basis for tomorrow's work. When your work grows directly into tomorrow, you will be able to stop one day and pick it up the next day exactly where you left off. If you can do this now, you are on target. If you cannot, you have to do a lot of leftover work.

Before asking for additional work, you must be up-to-date. There are larger and larger numbers of people on Earth asking for more work— and we are not impressed! We see so much work undone, yet none of those seeking additional work lift a hand to help clear the streams of debris or muck. When you clean up your life, you have the opportunity to clean up Earth, too. Do it!

The only one not upset about the world is you, if you are not *you*. When you see how much has been done to the Earth and your world by those disinterested in God, you will see why we grow impatient. There are a few ways you can do more and more—and get others to do their part, too. For example: Paint your house. If you paint your house, neighbors will paint theirs, too. One resident can change an entire area. Why? All people believe they are superior to someone!

If you believe you are superior to all you know, you believe your neighbors are unworthy of your time or respect, so you would not want your house to appear to be less than theirs. You keep up appearances in accordance with what others do. This is the human condition as it exists now.

What you do now to remain on Earth is of no interest to us as your teachers. However, we are here to learn why you prefer to sit and not enter the universe. We are not interested in when you left the last plane, or how many attempts you made to leave this one in the past, we are interested only in NOW!

The only way to leave your life behind is to finish it. Do it. Enjoy it. Go for it! Do all you came to do and more, but move to the next plane.

It is no big deal, but some say over and over again: *"I love this life and want to be here forever."* Stop saying it! It is not true, and it can hold you back.

The days before Tomorrow are these days—and these days are not NOW, rather *The Present*. Living now and *The Present* is all of Today. Once you go to bed it becomes yesterday and is forgotten. While you remain in that state of awareness, you can change all you do or rearrange it, but once you fall asleep, it becomes *you*.

This is your challenge: *Live today as if it will never be repeated or lived again.* This fact constantly escapes you! You believe you can repeat work or do over today what was done yesterday—and you cannot. Be aware of it when you go to bed, and make sure all is well within you then.

Few items in this world affect your afterlife, but some are the Bible, Koran, Bhagavad-Gita, and Book of Life—all of them. You cannot carry them with you into the next plane, but they help you know NOW. What do you need to know now? Why you are here and how to conduct yourself properly while here. These books are evidence that societies have passed beyond your ken, yet remain in the universe around you now.

You are unable to know if one scribe wrote them or not. The author of any book is not entirely alone when writing a particular book. Believe us about this, we know. We are involved in this particular writing in a very major way, but so are you!

Your mind fills in all the gaps where the written word stretches over and lets you follow. If you do not read it, there is no point in preaching or teaching it, so we let you decide which areas are most important to you. Why do you need to know which area is most important to you? You need to appreciate your life and see if the methods used here are agreeable to *you* or not. If they are, use them from now on. However, if you are aggravated or annoyed by any particular phrase, sentence, paragraph, chapter, or book, you are taking the right path to enter your most difficult period of growth.

You always resist what is not agreeable. Why? You do not want to work—and change always requires work!

If after reading about another who is very artificial (superficial), you said: *"What a terrible person! She or he is so artificial."* You told yourself: *'Why am I not like him or her? Why do I take everything so seriously? Why can't I enter life as lightly as others?'* This is baffling only if you never set yourself to the task of analyzing your motives. If you are accustomed to analyzing yourself, you are half-way to self-discovery. Doing something about what you discovered is what remains.

What you do in your spare time on Earth is of no concern to us, but important to *you*. Your time here is not long! Never long enough to do last-minute changes, so do not linger over trifles. Work on the big stuff first! If you have time left, do the little things that are fun and interesting to you or others.

This world would be seriously affected if everyone was not as full of life as they could be, which means you should enjoy being you and become all *you* came here to be. It does not mean you must play every day. Work for most people is more fun than play. Why? Play is pointless and devolves into less and less enjoyment, while work can evolve into the greatest life possible on Earth.

A few reading this book are too concerned about their work of the past. You need to let go of it and forget about what you should have done but did not do, since this harms your capacity to work now. Since Tomorrow will arrive tomorrow, your present life is what counts most.

The only person not upset by the world today is one just born into it. Why? That soul feels no responsibility for what declined prior to the moment of birth—all others do. You will see yourself become upset over crime, delinquency, ugliness, and costly waste of precious goods when you work and try to amass the fortune you feel entitled to now. Only then will you see how much everyone suffers for the greed of a small group who want everything for themselves.

Once you decide to change your life, you may decide others should change as you did. **Warning:** *Do not become a clanging gong!* If you are not to be attacked, resist the temptation to tell others how to live their lives.

The work of one person is not the same as anyone else's work—even if you all follow the same trade. Each person works differently, according to their lives in the past. If you lived many times on Earth before this life episode, you have a knack for working here, but may not realize it until you start doing it. Others may not be able to do something as well or as fast as you, and you believe it is their fault. You do not accept that you were given a gift from a previous existence that enables you to sprint forward and gain an edge on others this time. For this reason, you need to explore any advantage you have and develop each one now. Only then can you gain success at an early age and enjoy it all this life.

Keep the following needs in mind while you work:

1. You need to concentrate.
2. You need proper tools and a good attitude.
3. You need enough time to do the job right.
4. You need to be *you!*

These are basic rules—and as you learn more and more about working here, you will learn to use them all. You cannot skip over any of these four major points and succeed. If you work and follow each one, you will end up successful. We can guarantee it!

When You (The Higher Self) decides to end your career, you will know it. Life at work will not be fun. You will be easily irritated by all who refuse to appreciate the effort it takes for you to go to work or do it right. You may be out of sorts, perhaps even grow ill, but you will not die of work. Truly, no one ever died of hard work!

The unhappiest person in a workplace is the one who pretends to work but does not. There are any number of reasons why you might do that, but the most pronounced motive is: You are lazy. You must learn to motivate yourself!

You cannot expect people you work for to turn on your energy and creativity. That is your responsibility. The only way to avoid the life of a drudge is to make sure you do work you enjoy.

If the daily grind is just that, you need to add work after hours that inspires you or pays your needs. If you do not, you will lapse into the worst possible ways of life. You will go to work, come home, go to work, come home, go to work, ad infinitum, until this life is over. You will then have to return to work, because you did not make time to enjoy life here and now or learn to develop your other lives.

When we refer to *'other lives'* we usually are referring to lives lived on other planes, but you have other lives here on Earth, too. By permitting you to have more than one life, we can help you know if this life is good or not, but you have to keep them all straight.

There are seven ways you can be *you* and live seven different lives within one life while on Earth. We will itemize them and let you decide if you want to follow through and use this material or not. The decisions required here are always yours—never another's, not even God.

1. You will be asked to decide which of several different talents you wish to develop—and why. If you have many, you will be asked to

develop a few of them. If you decide not to do so, fine. You do not have to develop any talent.

2. You will be given a choice of using your talent now or later in life.

3. You may be *'called'* to a mission or not. If you are not called, you will be given no more help than others pursuing such work. If called, you trade one aspect of this dimension for another on this plane or above. This is why *'callings'* are rare.

4. The only way you can tell others you are here to do more is to first do it, then show what you have done. People never believe until they can see it—unless it is God talking to them.

5. You cannot help yourself, but can always do the work. Only when you cannot work will you be given help.

6. The end of one life blends and merges into the next if *you* let it.

7. The end of a life is never noticed in the universe.

These are seven different ways you can live now, but each builds upon the one before it. If you cannot advance beyond Step 1 or 2, you cannot reach Step 7. It is always your decision how far you go while here!

What you need now is time to develop into the fullest possible being you can be here, enjoying yourself as you grow. Before you can be of use to anyone else, you must know how to live and be yourself! If you cannot be yourself, because others expect you to conform to a pattern of their design and not yours, you can leave that atmosphere or environment without regret. Usually you hold yourself back far more than anyone else can or would even want to restrict you now.

Move your mind ahead in time and see if there are any others who might want to hold you back if you gave them the opportunity to do so. If you can detect someone wants to manipulate you into becoming their image or dream, you are wise to avoid such a situation or person. Be sure you do not try to manipulate others!

What you can do now is begin living this life and ending the life you had before discovering who you *really* are. If it takes you seven years to complete, fine. If it takes the rest of your life, you procrastinate too much. Some things cannot be changed easily due to problems associated with large units of life, but most can readily change simply by announcing your intention—then doing it.

The only World of Tomorrow you need to know about today is here—and going to be put to you now. What is it about Today that you need to work on—but have not? That will be your work of Tomorrow. If you finish it now, it will be complete and other work will appear, but right now this work is first on your agenda.

Being able to see into the future so you can manipulate events or people around you now is not a worthy ambition, but if you go that route anyway, you might as well learn how to do it correctly. Let us begin working to understand the mechanics behind such visions—so you can do it right.

The work of this world is not transparent to you, but obvious to many others. You cannot see through materials you use to build houses, walls, and factories, but they are not impenetrable. You may not know how to see through them, but it is not impossible to do so. You may not know how to walk through them, either, but it is possible. You only need to know how to do it. First, learn how to see the future!

Here is how you can see into the future:

1. First, put your hands flat on this page, then see if you can feel the printed words. Can you feel the letters rise under your fingertips? Do you know where the print lets off and clear page begins? You can teach your fingers to detect this difference. You may have to practice this a lot.

   Once you can tell the difference between one thickness and another, you are able to detect the difference between the layers of a plane. There are thousands and thousands of layers that can be separated from the millions that make up this plane.

2. Place your hands on your head—anywhere. Where did you place them? If you chose to place your hands on your nose, you tend to look forward. If you placed them on the back of your head, you always look back. If you placed them on top of your head, you look up. Those who always look back cannot see into the future, and those who always look forward cannot view the past, thus only those who look up can easily see into the future.

There are seven different types of people on Earth, and you are made up of one, two, or more types. If you are like the first group, you are selfish and inconsiderate of all, but will get ahead in this world. If you are more like the second group, you will be less selfish and more interested in what is going on all around you. You will not be as likely to succeed as the first group, but more likely to have friends.

The third, fourth, fifth, and sixth groups are not alike, but are more likely to get along with each other rather than with others. However, the sixth group is less likely to succeed than the fifth group, and the fifth group less likely than the fourth.

The seventh group can forget all of this world's ways and enter into its own work and prosper. Why not start out this life in the seventh group? You cannot! It takes years of work on Earth to get this high.

There are only two people who need your help—you and your inner self. If anyone near you also needs help, you start to feel cramped—maybe need air. If you are with others who are also doing their work and not expecting anything from you, you can breathe easily and laugh—and enjoy yourself.

Sometimes it is necessary to help others in order to learn why they are failing at life, but usually you do not help them—only limit their experience. Experience is what differs from one worker to another—not educational level attained, words spoken, or games played.

You are an organization, and to run any successful organization you need varying levels of expertise. If you are inept at everything, you learn nothing well and live from day-to-day. If you are experienced in one field, many elements of that job will override into other areas of life and help out when needed. If you never study, or others shield you from all of life's lessons, your expertise and knowledge are so limited that your self-esteem is unable to grow or develop beyond childhood—which is a pain for everyone else.

Work on doing this daily: Do your work and expect others to do their work. Help those temporarily out of work, but mind your time. If you start helping others who are not in need, your life will quickly show neglect in key areas. The ego likes to help others—even when they are not in need of it. Spirit knows better!

Work on the present
And your future will improve!

If you need an example of this wisdom, look at your day so far. You are now farther along the path to enjoyment of this life than when you started this chapter. Why? You are working hard and seeing immediate results. That is what good work does for you!

Your future life on Earth is not guaranteed, but if you diligently work and learn how to handle money, your prosperity is insured. Those two things are the basis of all this life's earned prosperity. Once you know this, you have access to more than you ever knew existed in this world.

Be ready to live and let live!

Free your life before helping others learn how to live. It is not your time to teach if you are still learning the basics. All teachers had to learn whatever they teach. However, you are not here to teach, but to learn. If you learn *all* your lessons, you will then be asked to teach as we do. Wait until you are asked, or your ego could lead you into strange and dangerous territory you are not equipped or prepared to delve into now.

Symbols are not the best way to identify Earth and its territory, rather a way to know which territory is safe. Be sure to identify your land first and learn about it, before you act like you own it. There are several other lands we will visit on this plane before we must leave, but right now more work has to be done on *The Present* before *The Future* can reveal itself. Be ready to work!

The next chapter is the most difficult chapter to date. We have not yet given you enough work to do, so we will add this thought now: *Work, work, work, and then work harder—before leaving this plane, so your next world will be shiny, new, and bright.*

You deserve a better life than this one!

Chapter Twenty

When you decide it is time to begin a new day, *let it be a new day!* Do everything that needs to be done—not just what you want to do, or you will end up being indebted to that day thereafter. If your work is unsatisfactory to *you*, you will not enjoy it or do it particularly well, but do it anyway.

The only way to know you are *you* is to work and do the best you can. If you cannot work, you have a long, hard life ahead of you here. Learn as soon as possible how to work and your life here will be easier.

What you teach a child is not working for you, but work for the child. A child's play is hard work in which he or she learns many skills. If you avoid teaching the child, the world will teach its lessons, and they can be harsh and cruel. Be sure you do what you obligated yourself to do when you brought forth a child—or you may be forced to return to Earth.

When you cannot decide if a child has a life of its own, or is involved in something you do not believe is good, you are the adult and are obligated to stop it. Any excuse to the contrary will not reduce or remove it. As a thinking, loving, helpful adult, you must do what you must do to help children, but do not do their work, for that will hinder their development and not help them in the end.

If you do everything you can for other people, you hurt your chances for success. Why? You are here to live this life as well as you possibly can and be ready to enter the next plane at the end of it. You have enough time, but you do not have much extra time to do everything.

If you rush around helping everyone you know do their work, you are egotistical and indeed saying, *"I'm great! I have all my work done, but you can't handle yours."* This may not be what you intended, but others see it that way.

Work on the difference between helping someone out of a difficult situation and doing their life work for them. One is an outstanding way to get ahead today, if they return the favor, but the other condemns people to having to repeat life's lessons until they learn them. To sidetrack another in the guise of helping them advance is the act of an enemy—not a friend.

What you need to do now is act like a friend, be a friend, and consistently do what friends do for friends. Do not act like a friend one time and an enemy on other occasions, or you will end up friendless. Others watch to see if you can be trusted, if you are sincere, and if you sincerely care. If you betray friends, relatives, superiors, or even strangers, all know you cannot be trusted and will withdraw from you.

These basic lessons in human relationships are being repeated now, because at this point you need a refresher. If you have no doubt now about who *you* are and where you are going, you are no longer a student but a teacher. We welcome all who are ready to teach, but we have a few ground rules—including how to teach, when to teach, and what to teach.

The above is a very concise review of what you need to know. Study it and make sure you understand it before going on to the next paragraph.

There are seven different types of people in your life now, and there are always going to be seven different types of people around you. Astrologers today say there are twelve types based on planets and months of the year contrived by man. You need to know there are only seven personality types.

When you deal with someone who is obviously not very intelligent, you must be wary, because most are extremely sly. Yes, there is a very strong bias against the less intelligent, and they are always aware of it. They have no real love of those above their level of understanding. If you work with or teach such people, be aware they will often undercut you and talk behind your back, because they fear you. They want to be considered smarter than they are, so they hurt those they fear are truly wiser or those the world respects.

What you need to know now in order to teach is a few basics on how to handle people who undercut your authority as a teacher. You need to know how to keep order and do the work of a leader without being seen doing it. The teacher is above the student in only one area— the one being taught at the moment. In all other areas a teacher is not held to know it all, so do not act as though you do.

What a student does is no reflection on you!

Each student is a total entity who will or will not accomplish what you teach and will or will not act according to what you believe is the proper way to behave. You are merely a guide and cannot force anyone to do what you think is best. In this way teachers are preparing to be Spiritual Guides on another plane and most likely to be selected at such time as those decisions are made. You need not worry about it now, but it is *preparation* that carries from one life episode to another.

If you have a large class, you cannot give each individual a lot of attention—which is the best way to teach many. If a student is overwhelmed, let that individual seek help. If a student is bored, let that one work on a project that interests or helps others, but do not let that student disrupt the class. You are in charge!

A large family is the basis of all communal life and is recommended to develop the best, well-rounded personality to its fullest potential. However, in these—the latter days, having large families is discouraged. You will possibly need to adapt the philosophy of the large family's parents to your smaller families.

It is helpful to remember that constantly watching over someone inhibits and often scares that person. If you wish to build self-esteem, let each child go and do everything humanly possible at that stage of life to teach needed skills and the meaning of life. They will learn well then!

When you ask another to do something for you, do you expect them to do it? Why? You need to observe others to a certain degree or you will never get anything done by them. If you never pay attention to other people as a general rule, hopefully you will never need anyone to help you. If your life is totally immersed in your own problems, you will not find anyone interested in you. You have to share a certain degree of your life with others, but a fine line must be drawn when it comes to acting upon another's advice. Keep in mind to not seek advice and then not follow it!

Let others live!

If you are prone to set others straight—as you see it, you will not let them finish a sentence let alone a life without interrupting them, trying to dull their sensations and feelings. Be true to *you*, but do not expect others to cater to you. Be fair. Love all!

This is the Law of God: Be true to *you!* You need not worry about others if you do all you should do. Others reflect your life back to you and repay you in kind.

What you do on Earth is not that different from other planes when it comes to certain areas of interaction with other souls. If you learned a long time ago to behave properly, you do it now without problems. If you cannot control yourself, you continue to learn much.

To reach teen years and not know how to feed, clothe, and clean your body is sad neglect by adults, but when it becomes your life and body, you are held responsible for doing these things as any adult does. You cannot continue to blame adults for bad behavior once you become one! You are totally responsible for your behavior then.

What if you were to wear a thin suit of clothes into a freezing cold room, would you freeze? Would you be upset enough to catch a cold?

Would you leave the room quickly? The best answer is obvious. If you continue wearing a thin suit, you would leave immediately. However, if told previously you should wear a heavy suit, and you chose not to do so, you will either freeze in the cold room or catch a cold. Such punishments are meant to teach wisdom.

Why learn lessons the hard way? Why not obey and comply with wisdom immediately? There is a lot in life you need to know before you can enter the next one, but most know it all by the time you reach your oldest age here—whether that is during your teen years or your nineties. What you need is a life plan that helps you learn sooner rather than later.

Begin your studies when young, and usually you will be ready for whatever happens in later life. If you let your studies wane and die early, you will learn lessons all of this life. Which plan is most practical and leads to the greatest success in this life? Obviously, if you are well-prepared earlier than others, you will gain success sooner than most.

When your life is on the wrong path or track, you cannot do much without feeling compelled to check and double-check your work. If you find such indecisiveness in all you do at home or work, or in personal relationships, you need to learn a few things immediately. Decisions based upon the best knowledge available to you at the time are always best. If you alter them or change your mind, you dilute the energy needed to confirm your decision. You may even cause them to fail. Be accurate and concise, then let go of the outcome. Your work will succeed if you do!

There are a few people disliked by others because they succeed at everything they try. Why do people hate them? Because they fear such people. They believe they will take over the world and leave nothing for the less talented to do. This is a mixture of greed and jealousy—and rampant today.

You need to recognize that God sent some here to help you. Why would you want to follow or be guided by idiots? Choose the best, and then let them go. Trust your judgment and let it flow. If your life does not flow in time, change the ingredients or the direction of the flow, but give it enough time to gain momentum.

Once you elect officials, be honest and let them do their jobs. Do not become jealous of them! The only one not jealous of another is the one who is superior at living this life.

If you do a large number of tasks very well, you will never be upset if others are also adept. If you are lazy, stupid, or unwilling to learn how to handle a large number of life's lessons well, you will resent all who do their work better than you. Why be jealous when you can work and do it yourself?

There are seven different reasons why you cannot do your work, but only one really matters: *You are not willing to do it!* That one reason stops all progress.

If you need to accomplish an important step in order to advance—a college diploma, for example, but neglect to do it, you cannot ask to be paid the same wages as those who complied with the world's demands for such a credential, regardless of whether or not you are more intelligent, skilled, or experienced. The qualifications of life are not the same as those for business. A business can object to your lifestyle and require different attributes. You decide if such a business is good for you and stick with it or leave. If unwilling to obey and comply with their rules, never complain about not getting to the top there.

The business world is not the only arena here on Earth where organization is everything. The animal kingdom is not a kingdom at all, rather an organization that develops itself, feeds itself, and gains new insights into how it can survive. You are no different. What you do to survive is little different than what you do to enjoy yourself, so incorporate the two and have a much happier existence now.

You obviously need to work; you need help to get further down the road than you can walk alone; and you are helpful by nature. Put them all together and explore which life plan best accommodates all these facets of your personality, then do whatever it takes to succeed. It will save you a lifetime of misery and defeat!

There are seven different people, reasons, and fears, but only one needed to derail you for life. Be sure you are not overcome by any one of them, even if only a few bother you at times. Life is a balancing act requiring precision and deftness handling all the lessons you came to Earth to learn—while living a good life. Most people can easily do it all, if they fear no one.

Fear is not the only reason you do nothing, but it hinders you from living life to the fullest now. If you fear being alone, all run to you and you cannot get anything done. If you fear being crowded out, all avoid you and you do not get enough interaction with others to know what the world needs now. If you fear something, the universal response is to supply it in abundance, which can limit your advancement and possibly harm you—so do not fear anything. Let life flow and meet everyone halfway.

What if you see something you want to buy, but do not have money in your purse? If you need it, the shopkeeper most assuredly will set it aside for you to buy when you get the money. If you need it right then, cash will be extended to you by someone. We guarantee it! You may have to work for it then and there, but you can get what you need.

Affairs of life are simple unless you are grasping, eager, or worried, then life becomes tiring and disagreeable. Be sure you need something before demanding it, so life can once again be in sync. You have all you need! If you do not, sit down and figure out why, then get it easily. Others help those who know what they want, but shun those who seek the easy way out of living this life. Learn the difference and be popular, successful, and always able to have what you need when you want it.

There are seven different kinds of places you need to visit while here, but you can only cover one trip at a time. Do not dread any of them or look forward to them. Live to the fullest all the time you are at any location, knowing you are home and safe wherever you are—even in the dentist's chair. It is a gift, but if you are wise and wish to live a stress-free life while on Earth, you can easily adopt it.

There are seven different places where you are not welcome, but you do not know it until you visit those spots. Why worry if you are not wanted by others? You have your dislikes, too, so be generous and realize others are the same as you—only some are nicer, wiser, better equipped for life, etc. than you are.

How you learn is what helps you develop—not the development process itself. The development of the brain occurs before a human or animal carrying the fetus is aware of the pregnancy. Why? Because it arrived first. If your brain is underdeveloped, you are, too.

You may not know you cannot do all you dream, because the brain can decide what it can and cannot do and refuse to cooperate with you. If your brain is fully-developed and you are well, you can always get more help from your mind. If your brain is damaged by accident or abuse, you will not be helped, and will be handicapped all this life. God helps the infirm, but not those who deliberately set out to handicap themselves.

What if your will power is gone and you have nothing to eat? Would you eat your body? No, you would not do that. Why? Your body would not let you do it. If you eat another body, you are doing it because your body demands you feed it and wishes to eat flesh.

The body is aware of the sacrifice of flesh, but may still require it. Do not confuse the mind by insisting that eating flesh always harms the body. Your body rejects vehemently anything it cannot tolerate. If you cast up flesh, you will not eat it again! If you enjoy eating meat, and it never causes suffering, you adapted to it and can eat it with ease, so do it!

You cannot force beliefs onto the body, nor can the body demand the mind to react to its needs. They each have their own role to play in the development of your life here on Earth. Both are instrumental in your success or failure as an organism. Use them, but do not confuse them!

Your mind may not agree on what your body wants and how to provide it, but it will figure it out. You may want sex, but the body cannot reach out and take it. The mind has to develop intricate methods of seduction to get what the body wants when it needs it to live well. If the mind becomes diverted or contorted by outside elements, the body may be unable to get what it wants and will cause upheavals in the mind. The mind does the same thing to the body! Check out what your body requires and what your mind wants and give them free rein and see what happens. You will be well taken care of, but your soul may not be satisfied!

If your soul is the seat of YOU, why would you neglect it during this life? You do, if you never sit and develop a place on Earth for *you* to live free of all fear and deprivation—or you refuse to meditate or pray. Why be here if you cannot enjoy it?

The soul is where you learn to live and develop all that is *you* while here, and where you are most comfortable. Live only within your mind and you will be constantly upset. Dwell only on bodily functions and be sick, or live with a clean heart, pure mind, and your soul free to become all it came here to be.

These are elementary lessons only, but all require that the teacher master them before anything can be taught to students. Work to detract from no one else while building your life and you will be pleased with all you do in life, and others will honor you for it. Live only for you while here and you will find no surcease from the pain and agony of being human.

Teaching is divinely inspired or not, but the effects on a class are human. If you expect others to change, you must be able to change—otherwise you cannot teach. No one believes anyone who is not well-versed in their life's lessons, but you do not need to share yours.

All people have difficult lives—*for them*, but your life is of little interest or use to others, unless they ask you about it. To stand and deliver a presentation geared to talking about your life, your success, your failures, your anything, is of little use to students. Be yourself, but do not reveal you unless a student is actively seeking to know who you are or why you are as you are. This leads to less and less egotism—which helps this world start growing again.

When you grow, shed your past and move forward unencumbered—full of enthusiasm. If your enthusiasm starts to wane, start looking for a new door. It will appear! Open it and move ahead!

Life is good if you use it wisely, but life is miserable if you owe people money—or anything. We work to help you get out of debt, so you can enjoy this life. You cannot enjoy life if you are unaware you have only one life to live now. Be able to know who you are and why you came here, and you will enjoy life. Be confused, upset, *addlepated* (sic) or whatever, and you stand to lose out on this life's experiences, with no successes to relay to others. You may even have to return to Earth to clean up the mess you left for others. If you remain cool, calm, and understanding of others, you will succeed—regardless of the handicaps you set up for yourself this life.

Chapter Twenty-One

This is the end of the world you always knew! Once you reach the next plane and ascend to the heights of this work, you will never again be in this world. You will never want to return or live here again, either.

'Now is The Time' to prepare for the next life—not at the end of this one life. If you arrive anywhere prepared, you advance much faster and further than if unprepared, so be ready! You seldom have a lot of time on your hands while on Earth. Why? Because you waste time if you have too much—and do the same with money. You fritter both away on unnecessary things and pastimes if you have too much of either.

You do not need a lot of money to live, but your imagination may require a larger salary or wage than you have in order to feel happy. Work on the time it takes you to enjoy one hour of peace and see if you can get into shape and stretch it to at least two hours, then to three hours. You will be sure you did a lot then.

If your life is full of time unspent on *you*, you resent those who make demands upon you; but it was you who misspent your time—not others. You are not the only one who needs time to be alone, so get together with those who also need time alone and do it together. Yes, you can go places and spend time alone with others. You do not need to talk every minute you are with someone else. You may feel you must fill every gap in every conversation, but it is the silences that count most. That is when you see how we communicate with each other.

You always say: *"Communication is the key to success,"* but never believe it for a minute. You believe you are successful because you can command the presence of others to hear you out, and you are so persuasive all like you and believe you should lead them. You are totally compelled to believe this by your ego, because in its own way your ego reigns supreme over all you do while on Earth, but it never exists again. Do not let this temporary vehicle decide your future for all time!

What you do while on Earth is not as important as why you do it. If your life is not as well-designed as it could be, you are totally at fault—not us or anyone else in the universe—and certainly not God. You decided to enter the Earth plane, so do what you came to do and do it well, or start your life over later and do your work then—adding what you must do for this life. You can waste your life on Earth or develop a life that lives and breathes and helps you ascend—this is THE decision of your life!

When you live on Earth, at times you live as a hermit and at other times as a gregarious personality. This balances your life here and makes you both introverted and extroverted—with neither aspect too noticeable. Why do that?

Extroverts scare others and introverts bore them! If you balance these aspects of your personality in order to entertain and amuse yourself as well as others, while learning all you came here to study, you could leave this plane believing your job was well done, but only if all who knew you are saddened to hear you no longer share this world with them. If even one who knew you is not saddened at your passing, you failed this lesson in balancing life here.

What if you died today?

You would not know it! You would be gone from this plane in a definite split-atomic second and not heard from until you had completed the work you must do to convert energy into the next stage of evolvement, but after that you could return—and maybe visit from time-to-time.

Do you wonder what happens when you die or cross over? Why? You are not there! You are gone and unable to know the exact moment or care about it. Why not let others arrange their lives while you take care of your transformation? You can do this only if all the details of your life were taken care of by you.

You will yearn to see old friends and children most, but there are those who wish to *'haunt'* some old enemies. It is not permitted. You will not be allowed to end your days on Earth haunting another or being haunted by anyone else. Your days are here and now, and you are to design a lifestyle that permits you to enjoy the entire time you are here without hindering those around you from enjoying their lives as well. If you harm anyone else or hinder them by not doing your share of necessary tasks, you will be harmed by another or hindered in some other way. It is the universal law.

What you do now is not as important to *you* as it is to the world. This world is not going to make it to The World of Tomorrow at the present rate of deterioration and dismay. All cry for help—and sorrow flows from too many hearts now. You must repair the damage now or rage will overflow all and consume your hearts.

When the soul cries out for help and does not receive it, the heart aches for a while and then reacts violently. You have seen the evidence of your rage and know this is true, but you cannot stop judging the rage of others. If you do something—anything to help someone else die or end their life, you are not helping them advance or be more successful. You ended your fear of death while promoting it in others and will have to pay the ultimate sacrifice—a long, endless procession of unrest and derision. You cannot play God!

There is a saying in your world that goes like this: *'If enjoying yourself now, you will soon be sad.'* Why would you believe such nonsense? Why would you even want to believe it? Why would you want to enjoy nothing in order to insure your life continues to be mediocre or miserable?

Think about your life and when you were last happy. What happened then? Nothing happened that would not have happened anyway, but you had a pleasant respite before your turn came up again. This is life! Enjoy the good, so the bad is not that bad.

Hate the life of a good person and you will never be able to leave the life of one who is not good. You cannot condemn anyone else while your life is not clear and good or is in a state of chaos, but you can rue the day you condemned anyone who follows in your footsteps—for you will be judged according to your rules. If you are not pure of heart, be sure you are tolerant or you may find yourself in the same hole you placed others.

There are seven different people inside you, but only one is in control at any one time. You need to learn to distinguish which is in control as early as possible in life so you can enjoy all aspects of your personality. If you must, run around and search out astrologers or psychiatrists to tell you the seven ways you are different, or let us do it for you, but do not make it the rule book of your life.

Life is not lived according to written rules!

Life is in the stars, or so some say, but the stars seldom say a word today. How can they? They exist in another world and have no knowledge of yours. Be realistic! Get into gear!

Work on your life and determine why you are as you are and let others do their work, too. Do not try to mimic static objects in order to learn who you are. Instead, live in an action-packed arena and know you are part of life.

Now to return to the seven distinct personality types—which fall into three categories and can be summed up into one. Here they are in order:

1. THE ATHLETE – The Athlete is not one who runs races or plays games, but the one in charge of maintaining your body. If you develop it, you have a lot of athletic ability, but may not practice

enough to earn prizes—but you still have it! You prize those who excel at all sports, because you recognize their determination and skill. Why? You do not wish to be as dedicated and do that much hard work, too.

2. THE VIRGIN – Every day you are here you are a virgin in some area of your life, but may not realize it now. You are afraid of things you have never done! Fear is what keeps you from trying to do new things. Recognizing you *are* afraid transforms you from a virgin to an accomplished player in life's games.

3. THE WHORE – If you ever sold out your dreams so another could do something for you—instead of doing it yourself, you are a whore. It can happen before the age of puberty, but most often when marriage is undertaken. This whore is not bought and paid—but accepts goods and security in exchange for physical presence. All can become whores! Greed is the biggest customer of whores and continues to dominate the world's business arena, but is seldom recognized as such now.

4. THE PROTECTOR – The punisher and protector of your life is not the athlete, the whore, or the virgin, but another totally different aspect of *you*. This is the source of all you fear. You can be totally safe, yet the protector can make you afraid. Why then seek out The Protector? You are inclined to let sentiment overrule mind at times and leave you defenseless. The Protector is there to alarm you and make you react.

5. THE CREATOR – This is the desire to own and create. You have the urge to create and raise a child of this life, but may not *really* want it. The instrument of life is a very serious implement and must never be allowed to fall into children's hands. They will permanently damage themselves and those who are carelessly thrown into the world by them.

6. THE GOOD *and* THE BAD – Yes, The Good *and* The Bad are ever-present in all who believe in God. The difference is one fears the other. The Good holds little regard for The Bad, but The Bad fears

The Good will tear them away from their lives or livelihoods here. You will never satisfy both sides of such a division, so early in life meld them together or become estranged from *you* forever.

The end result of all these variations on one theme produces:

7.   THE TOTAL YOU – 'The YOU of all *you* are' is never present in this life, but always exists. You can feel it when you harmonize and become attuned with all that exists through meditation, contemplation, song, prayer, or any other form of solitary refinement you choose to follow. You can never be all *you* can be, but it helps to at least try.

There are seven other aspects of life not as well known, but you can and should conquer them in order to believe you are not alone here and will be able to enter the next plane with ease. Try to remove the following phobias from your mind:

1.   Fear of Death
2.   Fear of Being Separated from Love
3.   Fear of The Future
4.   Fear of Being Revealed
5.   Fear of Distance
6.   Fearing The God of All
7.   Fear of Being You

You may wonder why *Fearing The God of All* is not last in line, but this life is one in which you are here to learn to be *you*—not become as frightened of God as you have been in past lives on Earth.

There are times in the past, present, and future when your Spiritual Guides and other workers in Spirit can help you research and develop a life that incorporates much *you* learned in earlier lives on Earth, but you cannot go back. You will be given '*gifts*' of spiritual work you earned in previous lives to enhance this life and help you do work more easily now—not to be used to amaze and baffle neighbors.

The work of The Holy Spirit is not that amazing to zealots, because they believe no one unlike them can be '*called*'. A terribly conceited misconception that leaves many in the dark at the end. You cannot help others, nor can you do their work for them, but you may be asked to offer assistance and help the masses as a whole. This is a totally different type of offering—one that requires unselfishness seldom found in The World of Today.

There are several people on Earth who are here to do something few ever did before, but they do not know of this calling yet. Why? Their humanity would operate against their accepting this call or being able to complete it.

When egotists are told about certain developments favoring them or promotion of their lives, they respond with enthusiasm and delight, but do not wish others to share in the outcome or be given similar advantages. We watch as gifts are given and observe the reaction of each person. If there is no deviation from their former practices, recipients may be given additional gifts. However, if 'giftees' (sic) are observed to overreach themselves or others, no further gifts are given—and what was given may be taken away.

Since many today are too literal in their work on wisdom, this requires a bit of explanation. For this reason, we insert here a proverb for you to think about:

When a man of prestige gives away his best work to another in order to help his tribe or others he leads, this is seen as greatness personified by all others in this work. Some on Earth may not agree and may believe this man is not sensible. Can you see how greed leaks into the belief system and creates different kinds of lies? You begin to doubt those who do good, instead praising evil-doers as men of God. How can you do this if wise? You cannot! However, some are given gifts from other lives that help them survive now. These gifts erase stupidity that may leak into their work today. Such gifts are of no use to anyone else and cannot be given away as a man of greatness might do without harming their individual opportunities to ascend.

There is no connection between the one who is gifted and the one who each step of the way earned wisdom, but the time involved is strikingly different. One may strive for thirty years to enjoy one single aspect of psychic development, then meet one who was given the gift seemingly overnight. Which is acceptable? Both are blessed and need to remain humble to possess such wisdom.

There is no other way to be here today and gone tomorrow except through death, so know that as long as you are here on Earth you will be here Tomorrow and unable to do anything about the end, except prepare for it. What if your life is never finished? You now realize the truth!

You are here for only a very, very brief episode of one total life of your entire being and will not be back again to repeat the exact same life and time. If you prepared for this time, you came on board ready to begin computer work, able to understand higher forms of math unknown earlier in the century, and able to decipher strange objects previously undetected by modern man. Why? You knew why then! You knew, because you chose this time and place before choosing the exact parental set-up or even the race or creed you would be born into this life.

If you now live and breathe electronics, remember you did not know anything about the subject until you were fairly old or learned it as a child. Now you know all about it—yet it has existed only a few years in this world. You have been gifted with prior knowledge! You were given advance information and are allowed to develop it now. If you are wise, you will help others not as gifted—or you become unable to leave this plane—or worse for the egoist, you may be surpassed in technology by all others.

The only day you know for sure you are here to do something for *you* is the day you find out who *you* are. If you never find out, you will never know! You have to design a life that lets you seek all *you* are, why *you* are, and why *you* came to Earth, so you have enough time to get ready for Tomorrow.

Tomorrow is here, but you do not know it yet! Computers were here long before this time arrived, and in other worlds, but your world was not interested in computers until Albert Einstein determined you could now use the information and technology. He was a saint of your modern times and a godly man. When he determined his theory was sound and others could understand it, the door opened to The NEW Age and The World of Tomorrow.

There are seven different people within you now, but only one is interacting with this material. Why let The Protector know you are unafraid? You have to control the urge to run whenever you see something new. You cannot develop quickly if after every new step or direction you must return to home base.

We welcome you! We will not harm you!

We will open the door to your life here, if you let us, but it is your ultimate decision that determines if you will rise above this earth plane or not. If you do, you earned the right to go forward and enter the upper planes. If you do not, you will repeat this life—and hopefully get it right the next time, if there is enough time.

The end of one book begins another, so we are ready to read what you think. If you enjoy this material, smile and laugh aloud now. If you fear it, please frown and say so immediately.

We can take criticism. We are not human. We love to laugh at ourselves, too, but we are not as serious about life as all on Earth appear to be. You must learn to let your inner self shine. Look at the sky more and enjoy the plane you are now on—hopefully for the last time.

We congratulate all now tired of studying The World of Tomorrow and anxious to get back to Today. You are now prepared to learn and live, and do not need to know more. You have all you need to live well now, but some will continue to want more and more information about the future in order to avoid living today. We will continue trying to help all of you ascend, but it is easier if students do all of their required work before asking for extra assignments.

The end of one paragraph begins the next until a chapter is finished, but one chapter ending does not necessarily mean another will begin. Be sure you close each chapter of life, in order to confidently step forward into the next one. That way, when you reach the end of this life you will fear nothing and know you are ready to leave this world—and Earth.

We fear you cannot let this book end or go forward to a new one if you do not know what to expect. Let this book be the beginning of your new life. Expect the next life to be much clearer and more enjoyable than this one. We will strive to do the same.

Work now—for the life of Today is the only one you have! Do not worry about The World of Tomorrow. It will take care of itself and be here when you are ready—not before.

Enjoy, enjoy, enjoy!
You deserve the best!

There is still one thing left undone. We recognize the fact that some words in this text are often misconstrued by editors to mean other than what we dictated, but forgive them because they mean well. *The Scribe* has done her work in accordance with our demands—and we are very demanding! We are teachers, after all, and this work is to be recognized as only part of life—what is not yet seen, but is always present.

We come to you now, but in future times you may come back to Earth or go to different places and times to teach and guide others or even relive a life. Be fair now and let everyone else know God is here and everywhere—and you are of God. Nothing more can be said by us now about The World of Tomorrow.

About **The Scribe**

To understand the role of Ruth Lee, Scribe for *The Teachers of the Higher Planes*, you need to know how her work differs from traditional scribes. She picks up intuitively what is constantly being channeled from sources within and beyond this universe to each of us in this world, instantaneously sorting through millions of incoming signals and their various links in order to *'trance-scribe'* spiritual works such as **The Books of Wisdom**. Her work enables you to easily read and quickly use our work in your daily life.

When ready to scribe such work, Ruth Lee enters an altered state of mind and lets her Divine source monitor the proceedings as she types rapidly. She can and often does simultaneously read the text aloud as it arrives in time—about as fast as most people deliver speeches. However, she retains no memory of such work, and when done writing must read it again in her usual state of mind to gain its full meaning. That is about all you can discover about this mystic Scribe now—the rest is a mystery!

For more information about **The Books of Wisdom**, *The Teachers of the Higher Planes* and Ruth Lee, Scribe
Visit: www.LeeWayPublishing.com

Have you read the other
Books of Wisdom?

There is more to living and dying than we can observe while living on Earth. However, many remain unaware that intelligent beings exist beyond our time and space. They work diligently to teach us universal truths so we may transcend this earth plane before Earth is destroyed by man.

We Are Here ~ *The Teachers of the Higher Planes*, the first volume of *The Books of Wisdom*, introduces the work of an elite group of entities charged with educating humanity about the basic facts of life, spirituality, and ascension. Their revelations are startling! In plain prose, *The Teachers* concentrate on addressing the fundamental questions of life, providing straight answers anyone can understand and use immediately.

The second volume in *The Books of Wisdom* series, **The Work Begins,** explores more deeply our illusions about this world and these times, urging us to pursue our spiritual work with greater vigor than ever before. *The Teachers* deliver the ways and means to escape calamities that might befall mankind if not ready to ascend at the end of this life and move to a higher plane.

The Art of Life ~ *Living Together in Harmony*, third volume in *The Books of Wisdom* series, covers in depth all relationships known to man. Finding love and being loved is just one area of the many covered. Each page explores relationships existing in this world and others—omitting nothing. So much is given, because love is a matter of relativity!

The fourth volume in *The Books of Wisdom* series, **Now is The Time,** came out in audio tape in 1996. Now you can read what thousands testified drastically changed their minds and lives. You cannot avoid the sense of urgency *The Teachers* project through this work! We do not have time to waste.

Bliss is It! completes the series in more ways than being the sixth and final volume of *The Books of Wisdom.* A jubilant, thrilling work of art from *The Teachers of the Higher Planes* that completes their work with *The Scribe.*

Ruth Lee, working as a spiritual scribe, enabled *The Teachers* to efficiently and easily dictate materials essential to our living full and meaningful lives here on Earth. Their work is revolutionary in its straight-forward presentation of facts the world needs to know in order to evolve ever higher, as well as help humanity achieve more advanced levels of love, success, and peace in every aspect of daily life.

You may wonder if these books should be read in any particular order. Only You (your Higher Self) can advise you, since each book is profound and delivers far-ranging wisdom exploring life on Earth. The wise will keep all of these scribed books nearby and refer to them daily, never tiring of learning and studying with *The Teachers of the Higher Planes.*

For more information, visit www.LeeWayPublishing.com

www.ingramcontent.com/pod-product-compliance
Lightning Source LLC
Chambersburg PA
CBHW052038090426
42739CB00010B/1956